THE COUNTERFEITER

and Other Stories

THE COUNTERFEITER

and Other Stories

Yasushi Inoue

Translated, with an introduction
by Leon Picon

TUTTLE PUBLISHING
Boston • Rutland, Vermont • Tokyo

This edition published in 2000 by Tuttle Publishing, an imprint of Periplus Editions (HK) Ltd., with editorial offices at 153 Milk Street, Boston, Massachusetts, 02109.

Copyright ©1965 by Tuttle Publishing

Cover photographs © Horace Bristol, "Fireworks over the Sumida River, Tokyo," ca. 1946-1956

Library of Congress Cataloging-in-Publication Data in Process
ISBN: 0-8048-3252-8

Distributed by

North America
Tuttle Publishing
Distribution Center
Airport Industrial Park
364 Innovation Drive
North Clarendon, VT 05759-9436
Tel: (802) 773-8930
Tel: (800) 526-2778
Fax: (802) 773-6993

Asia Pacific
Berkeley Books Pte Ltd
5 Little Road #08-01
Singapore 536983
Tel: (65) 280-1330
Fax: (65) 280-6290

Japan
Tuttle Publishing
RK Building, 2nd Floor
2-13-10 Shimo-Meguro, Meguro-Ku
Tokyo 153 0064
Tel: (03) 5437-0171
Tel: (03) 5437-0755

05 04 03 02 01 00   9 8 7 6 5 4 3 2 I

Printed in the United States of America

TABLE OF CONTENTS

HUMAN pathos and suffering, loneliness and isolation, Oriental fatalism and Buddhistic concepts of predestination form dominant strands in the fabric of virtually all of the writings of Yasushi Inoue. Probably his own separation from his parents when he was a child set the pattern for the basic framework of these moods, particularly that of loneliness. Here, it is perhaps interesting to note that the usual Japanese word for loneliness, *kodoku,* is made up of two Chinese characters—*ko,* "orphan" and *doku,* "alone." And Yasushi Inoue as a child was an "orphan alone" in almost every sense except the legal one.

Born in 1907 the son of an Army physician in Hokkaido, the northernmost of the four major islands that comprise Japan, Yasushi Inoue was taken during his infancy to live with his grandmother in a small village on the Izu Peninsula, some hundred and thirty-five miles south of Tokyo. This area is obviously dear to him; he calls it "my native Izu Peninsula" in *The Counterfeiter* and opens *Obasute* with references to his childhood there. One cannot help but feel that his delicate sensitivity to all natural beauty harks back to that time when separation from his family and personal loneliness led him, even as a child, to seek solace in Nature, which surrounded him in that mountain village. While separation and isolation strike gloomy chords throughout Inoue's works, it is to natural and other visual beauty that he inevitably turns for release, comfort, and meditation. It is one of the characteristics of his style to ease his readers down to earth again after the more dramatic sections of his stories by some gentle description of natural beauty.

This sensitivity to beauty appears to have been highly developed in the young Yasushi by the time he entered college and probably much before that. Although according to the dictates of filial duty he should have followed in his father's footsteps and become a doctor, science held no interest for him and he majored instead in aesthetics during his collegiate years at Kyoto University. It was probably during these years that the three persistent themes of the writings of Yasushi Inoue developed: a deep and abiding interest in Chinese history, stemming from his studies of Oriental art and particularly its Chinese antecedents; an ever-present consciousness of art and artists (many of his stories deal with artists and their works); and an involvement with social problems, present and past.

Inoue, who is one of Japan's most prolific writers today, started relatively late as a novelist. He was forty-two when he published in 1949 his first works, the two novelettes *Ryoju** and *The Bull Fight,* which the following year won for him the top literary prize in Japan, the Akutagawa Prize. His longer *Tiles of the Tempyo Era* (1957) deals both with art and ancient China; *Lou-Lan*** and *The Flood**** are short historical novels of China. Whether he is writing full novels, novelettes, or short stories, however, Inoue's penchant for detailed, ex-

* Two excellent English translations of this work have been published, one by George Saito entitled *Shotgun* in the collection *Modern Japanese Stories: An Anthology* and the other under the title *Hunting Gun,* by Sadamichi Yokoo and Sanford Goldstein.
** Edward G. Seidensticker's translation of *Lou-Lan* appeared in the *Japan Quarterly;* vol. VI, no. 4 (October-December, 1959).
*** This has been translated by John Bester and was published in the *Japan P.E.N. News,* No. 4, December, 1959.

haustive research and historical accuracy give his stories a flavor of authenticity. Even the characters in his stories can often be traced back to historical individuals. In the spring of 1964, Inoue went to the United States to start his research on what he personally believes will be his magnum opus, a multi-volume treatment of first, second, and third generation Japanese abroad, particularly in the United States.

Prior to his emergence as one of Japan's most prominent literary figures, Yasushi Inoue worked as a reporter for the *Mainichi Shimbun* in Osaka. In two of the stories in this book there are specific references to his employment as a newspaper man. One wonders if the dissatisfaction with newspaper work which he attributes to his brother in *Obasute* is not really autobiographical, for Yasushi did, as he relates in *The Counterfeiter*, resign from the *Mainichi Shimbun* and move to Tokyo shortly after his initial successes in literature with *Ryoju* and *The Bull Fight*. During the war, he did in fact move his family to Tottori Prefecture, the main setting for *The Counterfeiter*. There are a myriad of other authentic autobiographical references to himself, his childhood, career, and character in all three of the stories in this book. He attributes to Toyama in *The Full Moon* some of his own attitudes toward human destiny, attitudes shaped in both cases by separation from parents at an early age.

The impact of his own separation from his parents is a constantly recurrent subject to which he alludes directly or indirectly, for it had a powerful influence on his personal reflections and on his reactions to all mankind. In the beginning of *Obasute*, when speaking of his childhood, Inoue writes, " . . . but what I do recall in my faint memory is that my grandmother—or was it my mother? —anyhow, a member of my family . . ." came out onto a porch to comfort him. "Just a few words" of comfort, he writes, and one is impressed that the neglect he felt as a child has stayed with him, a haunting reminder of his isolation and loneliness. In all three of the stories in this volume, separation occurs: a husband from his wife, a child from a parent, a sister from a brother, a mother from her two children. These are sorrows which in Inoue's case are felt with deep intensity. They are coupled with cold and gloomy darkness, slag heaps, and shadows "like spilled ink"—an expression he uses in both *Obasute* and *The Full Moon.*

Inoue's training in aesthetics and his experience as a reporter would seem to have had marked influences on his style as a writer. Just as his work as a newspaper reporter was probably responsible for his lengthy research into detailed data before writing his stories, his exposure to Oriental art shows through in his descriptive powers. Like a *sumie*-painter who suggests forms with subtle brush-strokes, Inoue has a highly developed skill of portrayal through the least suggestion. His economy of language enables him to present intense drama and complex human involvement even in his shortest stories. But, even more, his characters ring true and are made real and vivid through just the slightest possible descriptive statements.

He wastes little or no time on the physical characteristics of the figures in his stories, and even his references to their personalities are generally encompassed in a single sentence, a phrase or a word. Of course, this sometimes has engendered the criticism that he tends to deal in stereotypes. Yet, even if he evokes stereotypic images, this technique in itself adds further credence and reliability to the authentic situations with which he deals. Inoue is one of the most precise writers in contemporary Japan. Given the lack of precision in the Japanese language itself, the precision in his choice of words is quite astounding. Stylistically, two main currents are constantly at work in his writings: a tendency toward long, involved descriptive sentences, with a host of modifying clauses and phrases each of which has its clearly directed purpose of elaboration of detail, and a tendency toward the compactness of individual phrases characteristic of Japanese poetry. Inoue, in fact, had aspirations of becoming a poet before his success as a prose writer, but he freely admits to failure as a poet. Be that as it may, if economy of words is one of the prerequisites for good poetry, in that respect much that is contained in Inoue's fiction is poetry of the highest order, but unhampered by the tyranny of form that pervades so much of Japanese culture.

The three stories assembled here reveal yet another facet of Yasushi Inoue—his great compassion for his fellow human being. The tragic Hosen Hara in *The Counterfeiter* and the pathetic Kagebayashi of *The Full Moon* are not particularly pleasant people by any standards, Oriental or Western, but the sympathetic compassion with which Inoue handles them provides a real insight into the nature of the author. It therefore seems rather surprising to find in *Obasute* that Inoue harbors a fear that "misanthropic blood" possibly flows through his veins.

Finally, a word or two about these translations and the subject of translation itself. For some years a battle has been raging among the critics of translations regarding the functions of the translator and the liberties he may take with the language of the author's original work. On one side of this argument, there are those who challenge even slight deviations from the original and condemn the translator who departs at all from a literal rendition of the author's lines. On the other side, there is the group of translators themselves, and a few critics who support them, who wander rather far afield in trying to render the author's thoughts, his language, and his imagery in a more palatable form for the Western reader.

This argument is not unique to the translation of Japanese literature, nor is it an argument that belongs only to modern times. One need only recall the various approaches to the translation of the Bible to realize how eternal this controversy is. The translations in this volume lie somewhere between the extremes of the two schools of thought. If anything, they tend toward literal renditions, and a purposeful attempt has been made to adhere as closely as possible to Inoue's originals. Some liberties have admittedly been taken, however; some of Inoue's long involved sentences have been broken up into two, three, or sometimes even more, sentences. An attempt has also been made to keep footnotes to a minimum because of a fear that they may detract from the flow of Inoue's language. As a result, it has at times been necessary to induce some descriptive language and circumlocutions to help the Westerner with words or situations that are peculiarly Japanese. In general, however, a conscientious effort has been made to present Inoue's stories in their original form, preserving their inherently Japanese character and tone with a minimum of departures from the original flavor. With the exception of these few explanatory departures, where deviations from the originals may have crept in, they should be blamed on the translator's misinterpretation of the text rather than purposeful distortions.

LEON PICON

THE COUNTERFEITER

THE COUNTERFEITER
(Aru Gisakka no Shogai)

I

ALMOST ten years have elapsed since I was commissioned by the family of the Japanese artist Keigaku Onuki to undertake the job of compiling Keigaku's biography, but I still have not fulfilled the contract. This spring I received from his family in Kyoto one of those printed announcements, with reply-postcard attached, inviting me to attend memorial services at a certain Zen temple commemorating the thirteenth anniversary of Keigaku's death. Frankly, I found it a bit difficult to face Onuki's people at that time. Unfortunately, or fortunately, I couldn't attend the services because of my work. But, the fact of the matter is that I was rather relieved that I *actually* could not attend.

When the contract for compiling Keigaku's biography was first negotiated by Onuki's heir, Takuhiko—I think that was around 1942—the original understanding was that there was no particular hurry about completing it. On the other hand, he had implied that he would like to distribute copies, as an offering to the spirit of the departed, to those who attended the seventh memorial services, so he wanted to have the work completed in time for publication prior to that occasion. The seventh anniversary was to be commemorated in April 1945, the year the war ended, and the feverish pace of life toward the end of the war was confused enough for both the Onuki family and me, even without Keigaku's biography. Consequently, my work on the biography

15

reached a state of temporary suspension while I was still in the process of collecting material, and although I hadn't actually abandoned the project, my contract came to a natural dissolution. As it happened, the contract was renegotiated by the Onuki family after the war. They said that now that normalcy was returning, they couldn't wait and wanted me to complete the biography as soon as possible. So ever since then I have been getting postcards from Takuhiko, roughly once a year, asking about the status of my progress on the biography and hinting pointedly at the desirability of speed. At such times, in desperation, I have been forced to fabricate excuses in order to placate him.

Originally, I had been selected for the onerous task of doing Keigaku's biography for a variety of reasons. At that time I was a fine-arts reporter for one of the Osaka newspapers, and in the course of my work I had met with the late artist on many occasions. It seems also that the late Keigaku had held me in higher esteem than he held the reporters of other papers. There were all sorts of factors like that. Additionally, I was selected by the Onuki family and by Keigaku's disciples because they felt that since I was the most competent person to undertake the biography, it would be relatively easy for me to collect material. Also, as a fine-arts reporter with somewhat of a store of knowledge of the artistic world, my point of view was likely to be bought.

When I was first approached, I had jumped at the opportunity of taking on this arduous task. I was very fond not only of Keigaku's work but also of Keigaku as an individual. Besides, compiling a biography of Keigaku would be more than just writing a history of Kyoto's art circles with him at the core; it would be like writing a history of Japan's art world. I thought it would not be a bad idea at all to seize this once-in-a-lifetime opportunity for me, a reporter, to do a study of the transition

and change in Japan's art world from the Meiji period*
on.

On taking a second hard look at the job, however, I
found that it was not going to be as simple as I had
thought. In the first place, one had to start from the
beginning by drawing up a chronology. Before construct-
ing the magnificent Kyoto mansion in which he lived in
his declining years, Keigaku had changed his residence
in and around Kyoto more than ten times—as his mood
suited him. And, also as his mood suited him, for half
of each year he was in a state of constant travel. Thus
it was difficult to ascertain when, where, and at which
ateliers his works, so publicized throughout the world,
had been produced. Moreover, as I started to trace the
course of his actions during a career of more than sixty
years and tried to reconcile the contradictory stories of
him told by all sorts of artists, disciples, art dealers, and
exhibitors, the job turned out to be not so simple as it
had appeared from the outside.

Another thing:

When Keigaku was fifty years old, he buried the wife
who had been with him through thick and thin over the
years. Thereafter, he lived with an aged housemaid
who survived him by two years. He also always had
one or another student staying with him, but these
students were constantly shifting, unable to tolerate
Keigaku very long because of his volatile personality.
The one person who should have known the late artist's
movements and actions best, his heir, Takuhiko, had lived
in France for a long time and had only returned to Japan
five years before Keigaku died. But he kept a separate
house in Tokyo, and since he was a sort of eccentric
egotist, as might be expected, he had almost no contact
with Keigaku's way of life. Thus, it might be said that

* 1868–1912: the period of the reign of Emperor Meiji.

there was practically no one who possessed a detailed knowledge of Keigaku's private life. To all this, one more thing must be added—and this follows from the nature of Keigaku's independent, extravagant, and rustic character—he always frowned upon what we call The Art Circles and lived consistently isolated from the artistic world. Because of this, I encountered tremendous difficulties and obstacles when I reached the point of collecting the materials for his biography.

For all of these reasons, I was unable to proceed with any expedition even as far as a draft of the chronology, which I consider basic to any biography. After visiting town after town on the Inland Sea coast near his birthplace, where his earliest work was done, and after going to see the small cottage-industry villages of Hokuriku, where, curiously, Keigaku enthusiasts were concentrated and had assembled those masterpieces of his later years that he had produced for sale, I was scarcely able to fill two or three notebooks with notes. Then, as the war increased in intensity, I had to drop my work on the biography while I was still in the midst of the basic research.

After the war, this backbreaking but delicate and tantalizing job again stared me in the face. Whenever I began to feel that I really had to get started on what I had committed myself to, the mere knowledge of the peculiar delicacy of this job kept me from feeling that I would now be able to apply myself to the task with ease. Besides—and this was a matter of some fundamental importance to me personally—I unexpectedly quit the newspaper after the war, went up to Tokyo, and turned my attention to literature. Completely immersed in this new kind of work, and with the chronology incomplete and full of gaps, I kept procrastinating, with the inevitable result that my work on Keigaku's biography simply remained in the form of those two or three tablets of notes.

That's the way things went. Even so, when it turned out that the biography wouldn't even be ready by the thirteenth anniversary, and considering the fact that I had delayed so long after having undertaken the job, I couldn't face the Onuki family. With the announcement of this memorial service staring at me, I resolved that this year I would really have to do something. I would try to assemble my work on the biography and put it into some presentable even if unpolished form and finally get this thing off my back.

So, because my own work efficiency is habitually not very great in the heat of July and August anyhow, I determined that I would spend these two summer months working on the compilation of the Keigaku biography. To that end, I took as a working place a small retreat in a mountain village at the foot of Mount Amagi in my native Izu Peninsula. There I decided to devote every morning to this job, and if I ran across some obscure points or situations, I would go to Kyoto in the fall to clear them up. At any rate, I proposed to complete a tentative draft and by some manner or means get the job done.

I must say that work progressed rather smoothly during July. By scanning almost ten volumes of his essays and travel accounts, I was able to complete my notes on his travels and the principal works he produced at each of these locales and when he did them. Thus, I was able to finish the draft chronology, albeit only in rough outline. As a result, upon entering the month of August, I was ready to adopt a writing approach by which I could pull together those facts and data that could be confirmed and discard everything that appeared conjectural. Referring to my old notes, I completed the writing of the sections of the biography: from his infancy to his youth; how he studied successively in Kyoto under Isso Katakura, Gaho Yoshimizu, and others; how he received honorable mention for presenting his debut-work, "Lost Happiness," at the 1897 Artists' Exhibition; how, availing himself of this opportunity, he had started to build his reputation as an incomparably brilliant artistic genius; and how he successively presented the works that have been praised as the masterpieces of his early period, "White Night," "The Old Fox," "Light Snow," etc. But here, my pen suddenly came to a dead halt. In narrating the period when the young Keigaku was blossoming forth as a colorful artist, I had been interspersing here and there the unedited contents of an unpublished contemporary diary, something in his own handwriting which could be considered unique Keigaku memorabilia. That diary had been turned over to me when I first visited the Onuki family after the war. It had been discovered together with various and sundry scraps in a Chinese bag which was in the Onuki family's godown when they were evacuating during the war. It was given to me by Takuhiko, who had said, "We've found something rather rare. I wonder if you don't need it for reference." On Japanese paper, in small characters, daily events from the end of 1897 to the summer of 1899 had been chronicled in fragmentary handwritten personal memoranda. For understanding Keigaku at that time, this was material that could be termed unique, unequaled and priceless.

What interested me most keenly in this diary was the discovery that this proud and arrogant genius of a painter, who was believed to have been without a single friend throughout his life, actually did have a friend called Shinozaki during this period. The name of this Shinozaki appears in three places, but Shinozaki is the only person except for members of the family who appears in this diary.

"With the silver trophy in hand, visit Shinozaki at Kitano; drink sake and chat with him till the wee hours," is one passage.

There is evidence, practically substantiated in earlier and later texts, that this refers to the time when he carried off the Special Award at the Kyoto Artists' Association Exhibition for painting "The Peacock." It would seem that in all likelihood he had taken the silver trophy with him and had gone to spend the night drinking and rejoicing with an intimate friend. Now, it is not difficult to imagine that this night was young Keigaku's most triumphant hour, and when you think about the fact that he was without restraint sharing that moment of glory with someone, you must look upon this Shinozaki person as someone who was decidedly intimate with Keigaku.

Next, there was:

"Am presented with a sea-bream by Shinozaki in the way of congratulations. Immediately go to visit Shinozaki at Shimota-chiuri,* but he is out. Leave something in large characters on the door and return home."

This, too, can in all probability be interpreted as meaning that after having captured the prize at some sort of exhibition and on being given a sea-bream as a congratulatory gift by this Shinozaki fellow, he had been touched by this token of friendship and had gone to call on Shinozaki at his home or boarding-house. The expression *"Leave something in large characters at the door and return home"* does not clearly specify what was written. But, it would seem that either in order to explain the purpose of his visit or to express his thanks, he had, as he did so often in later years, written a Chinese poem or some impromptu verse because he had been

* A section of Kyoto.

presented with something as a congratulatory gift. It may possibly seem an extremely rash thing for me to say, but that action left a deep impression on me as being one of the most truly graphic descriptions of the artistic genius Keigaku in his youth. The date is not recorded.

Finally, the one other passage in which Shinozaki's name appears is, *"Shinozaki left Shoyama this morning and came to Kyoto."* This passage is in the last section of the diary and is dated August 3, Summer 1899. This statement standing by itself can only be interpolated. This one line cannot be regarded as related to anything before or after or as having any special significance. However, at that moment when I first saw the place-name Shoyama, the very fact that a certain Shinozaki appeared to have been Keigaku's most intimate friend suddenly caused an image of the counterfeiter Hosen Hara to flash across my mind.

I had a certain amount of knowledge of this man Hosen Hara, who had spent his gloomy and miserable life painting forgeries of Keigaku's works. But when I realized that this person, who had remained dormant in my mind until that instant, was identifiable with this Shinozaki and that he could be considered Keigaku's only intimate friend during his youth, I was struck with an indescribably weird feeling.

Of course, this is something that had not occurred to me until then, but I did recall hearing at one time that Hosen Hara, if he can be called that, was adopted. In Hosen Hara's small native hamlet, situated on the Hino River which runs through the Chugoku mountain range, there are many people who bear the surname Shinozaki. Although I had never inquired about Hara's original surname, by putting two and two together I was able very early to arrive at the indisputable fact that this Shinozaki person and Hosen Hara were one and the same.

For two days I laid aside my pen and postponed the

task of chronicling Keigaku Onuki's biography. I passed the time idly, sitting in a wicker chair on the veranda, facing south and gazing at the late-summer Amagi mountainside as the sunbeams were rapidly fading. My thoughts turned away from the image of the brilliant early days of the artistic genius Keigaku, and Hosen Hara's hapless career captured my thoughts. Then, for the first time, all my fragmentary bits of knowledge of him fell into place, and it was a composite picture of his life that now flashed into my mind. Filled with a strong impulse to think further about Hosen Hara, I turned my face toward the mountain. There was something compelling in Hosen Hara's life that forced me to think about him.

II

IN THE fall of 1943, I had set out with Takuhiko Onuki to take a look at some of Keigaku's representative early works which had been produced and still remained scattered in various villages near the artist's birthplace around the Inland Sea in Hyogo and Okayama Prefectures. This was the first time that I encountered the name of Hosen Hara.

We had set a period of five days to visit the homes of the collectors of Keigaku's works and had scheduled our trip in this order: Akashi, Kakogawa, Takasago, Himeji, Shikama, Aioi, Wake, and Saidaiji. Since Takuhiko had generally announced in advance that we were going to make these visits, we were hospitably received at most of the houses, and we were able to inspect many works of Keigaku's second decade, hitherto known to us only by name.

While we were quite busily getting on and off trains,

the autumn sunbeams were scattered like fallen petals over the whitish sand characteristic of these places. As we got off at the small stations in the Harima-Bizen area, we had the feeling of being somewhere near the sea. We wandered about from house to house visiting the old homes and rich mansions of those who had been, in a sense, patrons of the late Keigaku, men who were written up in my notes. Because of our tight schedule, we had just one or two hours at some places. But even when we could have been more relaxed, I had to go half-galloping after the impetuous Takuhiko along the long pine-wooded roads and through the mud-walled residential areas. The late fall temperature was ideal, neither too hot nor too cold, but traveling at such a pace, our bodies were covered with a light perspiration. It had been my main purpose on this trip to see these works, and it was Takuhiko's intention to pay his respects at the homes of his late father's powerful supporters. But at each of those homes, we had to listen to one or two anecdotes about Keigaku's early days, and occasionally, if there were scrolls in unauthenticated boxes, Takuhiko was asked to autograph them.

Takuhiko, whose resemblance to his father was manifest in the high-strung temperament that showed in his face, thick eyebrows, and crewcut hair, would say, "Fine, let's do it!"

And he would roll up his sleeves to his big-boned shoulders, not at all like "a fellow who did as he pleased in Paris and whose charm and polish were renowned throughout the world," as he often boasted, and he would show that he could write characters surprisingly like his father's.

From the time of our first encounter, I had taken a curiously great interest in this contemporary of mine, this Keigaku the Second, and in a short time we had built up a frank, candid, and friendly relationship. Although he had been something of a profligate abroad, playing around did not interest him after he returned to Japan. As if his personality had suddenly changed, he did not care about either his reputation or his appearance. He gave the impression of staring wide-eyed at war-ravaged Japan, like a foreigner. Coupled with his defiant nature as a second-generation genius, he had the good-natured attitude generally attributed to young men from good homes. Rumors that had reached my ears before I actually met him were incredibly far from the truth. It seemed as though he was being stereotyped through misunderstandings of the nature of a son of a well-known painter.

He had inherited a prodigious artistic talent from his father, but gossip had it that he was lazy, shiftless, and incompetent, that he was slovenly and undignified, and he was rumored to be an offensive, despicable playboy. While it could be said that he had a profession—he was an engraver—he actually didn't do much of anything. There was nothing compelling him to do anything, because he had inherited an enormous fortune, a magnificent town house, and a villa, all bequeathed by his father. Before the war ended in defeat, producing his father's biography and collecting his father's most magnificent works had been the most compelling jobs for him.

In the course of my five-day journey with this Taku-hiko Onuki, we stumbled upon one fact of completely unanticipated interest. As if by prearrangement, one forgery of Keigaku's work had been collected at almost every house.

The first forgery of Keigaku's work that we encountered was in Kakogawa, at the home of a Mr. M——, one of the artist's patrons, where the head of the household had passed away some time ago. In the inner drawing room, which looked out over a well-kept garden, we were shown any number of Keigaku's works, among which there was one miniature, a scroll in the *Chagake* style which usually adorns tea-ceremony rooms. The scroll was labelled "North Kyoto Autumn Scenery." The instant that this one was displayed, I could tell beyond question what it was. Even Takuhiko, who had been peering at it from a vantage point off on the side, immediately turned his eyes toward me. Our glances instinctively met and intertwined.

"What do you think?" his eyes were saying.

For my part, I knew the original of this same work, which was held by a collector in Kyoto. Although Takuhiko had never seen it before, he knew instinctively from its lack of dignity and grace that this was not Keigaku's. He explained this to me later. At any rate, by checking with photographs in exhibition catalogues and other reference works, we could tell definitely that this painting had been drawn in imitation of Keigaku's work. As an extra precaution, right then and there, we opened a book of impressions of Keigaku's seals and checked. It seemed quite clear that in place of the stone seal always used with Keigaku's professional name, *Tekishintei,* a counterfeit wooden seal had been substituted. At first glance, the seal impression was a perfect facsimile, but on comparison with the two together, there were distinct discrepancies. Besides, the vermillion inking-pad that was used was different from the pads used in originals. Also, while the painting was furnished with an autographed case, this too was, of course, a counterfeit. When asked, the widow of the deceased owner said that she was acquainted with the man from whom her husband had acquired it; that he was a Japanese painter who carried old curios around with him; that she didn't know what he was doing now, but at that time he had briefly been living in Kakogawa; that he was a friend of Keigaku's called Hosen Hara.

When Takuhiko heard this, he exclaimed, "Did you

say Hosen Hara! I know him too. Let's see. . . when was that? At any rate, I vaguely remember meeting him two or three times when I was small. He certainly was a friend of my father's, and he used to come around to our house, but I once heard that he later became a counterfeiter of my father's works and my father forbade him to come again. So, that really was true!"

From then on, following upon the case of Mr. M——of Kakogawa, wherever we went, day after day, we found "Keigakus"—painted by Hosen Hara.

"This is another Hara-Keigaku, isn't it?"

"Beautifully done. Better than the original."

We continually engaged in exchanges of conversation like this, and though it was rather painful to the collectors, whenever we found forgeries, we exposed them as such. Some of them revealed themselves as forgeries at just a cursory glance, but at times there were works that were counterfeited in astoundingly exquisite and accurate detail. There were ways of identifying the forgeries because Keigaku originals had an air of artistic splendor and worth, but even beyond that, when we subjected some of the forgeries to close scrutiny, we found that they contained really gross errors here and there.

For example:

From his middle period on, Keigaku never used any whitish green in daubing his portrayals of moss and grass or rocks and crags, so forgeries which overlooked this fact or contained errors like this could be spotted at a glance. Further, a clumsiness was detectable in the forgeries when it came to the special way of using ultramarine at the bottom part of the white snow on Mount Fuji in summer, which Keigaku loved to portray. In all cases, evidence like this was available, and so the forgeries exposed themselves as forgeries.

All of the forgeries we saw had been acquired by the very same means and were by the brush of Hosen Hara.

Apparently this Hara was a very ingenious man. There were instances in which the art work, the artist's signature, the seal, and everything up to the autographed case could, as a matter of course, be ascribed to Hosen himself. Among the ten or so forgeries which we saw during this trip, only two could be considered to have been done in association with a bogus country art dealer.

Hosen had been able to gain people's confidence by claiming a close personal relationship with Keigaku—and this was a trump card he always used with buyers. On top of that, there were many cases in which he would tell the buyer whether he had gotten a particular item from Keigaku or had bought it cheaply, and then proceeded to palm off a forgery. There were also cases of his saying, among other things, that he would request Keigaku to do a picture on order, and after settling on an appropriate time for delivery, he would deliver.

The fact that he used as a middleman a dishonest art dealer whose character no one knew—and there were two definite cases of this—shows that Hosen associated with crafty art dealers, and this seemed worse than his just engaging in this kind of illicit work.

On this trip we half-jokingly began to bestow upon Hosen Hara names like "Keigaku-Hara" and "Uncle Hosen." We had uncovered some ten forgeries that he had produced, and from the collectors' stories we had obtained some fragmentary bits of knowledge about Hosen, but all of these stories concerned Hosen at the age of forty or fifty. That was a period when he changed his residence from place to place, wandering about as an obscure local painter. But, beyond what could be conjectured from Takuhiko's faint recollections, there was no way of knowing to what extent he had really had a close friendship with Keigaku. When we tried to synthesize the stories of all the victims on whom Hosen had foisted forgeries, we gathered that he had lived for varying periods of time in the small cities that we had visited along the Inland Sea, but he had not settled down in any one place for as long as five years. Since he was the kind of fellow who went around selling forgeries at will, inevitably, after two or three years had passed, there would be some sort of incident so that he could not earn a living or remain in any one town and had to move on to another place. However, he always moved to other small cities that were very close by, because he would have had a hard time earning a living if he had left the places where the Keigaku enthusiasts were concentrated.

Hosen did not introduce his wife to anyone except one person, a Mr. S——, the proprietor of a saké-manufacturing company in Wake. The story goes that several times Hosen took his small but beautiful wife for visits at this person's house and that he had, to a surprising degree, commanded the trust of Mr. S——'s father.

"I think Hosen was much more an art dealer than a man who painted pictures himself. I don't remember him very well because I was just a child, but it seems to me that when my father ordered paintings from Tokyo, he ordered them through Hosen. I'd guess that most of the things in this house were acquired with his help." These were the words of the current master of the house, a forty-year-old former university rugby star who didn't have much interest in the paintings. "I think that whatever he did he did well. That's because he was an engraver. Undoubtedly we must have something in the house that Hosen engraved."

Then he searched for it, but it was nowhere to be found.

We were shown some of the works by famous Tokyo artists that the former owner had acquired with Hosen's help. They were all genuine originals, and among them there were some small but rather interesting masterpieces that are very rarely found in country places like that. Considered in this light, there apparently was another side to Hosen that brought him respectability and trust among the Tokyo artists.

"In the final analysis," Takuhiko said, "Hosen is a Keigaku specialist. But even more, he manoeuvers with discretion and doesn't palm off more than one forgery per house." Actually, he was just like that. He could be regarded as a very clever and careful man.

It would appear from our investigations that for some reason Hosen lived in Kakogawa twice. The second time was when he was past his mid-fifties. At the end of that second period of residence in Kakogawa, in 1927 or 1928, he seems to have vanished from this area.

On the fifth and final day of this trip, returning from Saidaiji, we stopped near the Himeji coast and took up lodging at a small inn whose name I don't remember. It was our intention to settle down to recover from the fatigue of the five-day journey and eat some fresh fish. As we entered the room to which we were assigned, to our surprise we discovered in the *tokonoma** a landscape painting done by Hosen. It was a weird discovery. The artist's name, "Hosen," was written calligraphically in nearly square, easily legible characters, and the scroll was autographed with two seal impressions, *"Kankotei"* and "Hosen." Perhaps it was because we were so tired from our trip that this strange, fortuitous encounter with a work by Hosen made us feel so odd.

---

* The *tokonoma* has no Western counterpart. It is a long, narrow alcove or recess in a room (usually the main room of a house, but sometimes also the tea-room or master bedroom) used decoratively for displaying a prized hanging scroll. Generally, it is very simply and tastefully arranged with just the scroll and a flower arrangement or statuette. Every guest room at a Japanese inn has a *tokonoma*.

Takuhiko said, "We seem to be having rather close relations with Master Painter Hosen."

"This time he's revealed *himself*. I'd be surprised if this weren't a forgery of Hosen's work."

Both of us just stood engaging in that sort of idle chatter and staring at the scroll in the *tokonoma*. Actually, we had seen some ten Keigaku forgeries counterfeited by Hosen, but this was the first time for us to see his own work properly ascribed to him in his own name.

"It's not bad at all, huh?"

With an expression on his face that revealed his surprise Takuhiko said, "It could get Academy recognition."

To tell the truth, it *was* different, not in the least the sort of absurd art of dubious authorship that one usually finds in the *tokonoma* of these lodging houses. The subject, the corner of a high mountain enveloped in mist, drawn in the style of the southern painters, was quite commonplace, but it was drawn with minute precision and bore Hosen's own signature; and as we looked at it, it strangely permeated our minds.

"It has a peculiar spirit," Takuhiko said then. There certainly was something in the picture that had a peculiar spirit. For eyes that had just witnessed so many Keigaku masterpieces, this painting of course could not compete, but yet there was a spirit of destitution and solitude which had disciplined the work.

"*Kankotei,* indeed!" Takuhiko burst out a little later, as though he had been deeply impressed by something. He stared at the scene again and then walked over to the rattan chair on the porch. The sight of the Chinese character for "cold"—*Kan*—in that name and even the sound of that expression in my mind as I heard it sent chills through me, matching the eerie sensation that was inherent in the work.

That evening, we spent the last night of our trip

opening saké bottles. And under these circumstances, stories about Hosen were apt to prevail over the stories about the masterpieces of Keigaku's early period which we had been investigating all week long.

By some manner or means, the conclusion that we reached between us was that having painted such a picture as we saw there, Hosen could not be called completely devoid of talent.

"How foolish! Instead of the monotonous drudgery of forging my father's works, wouldn't he have done better painting pictures of his own?" Takuhiko, glancing wide-eyed at the scroll in the *tokonoma*, rolled up the sleeves of his *yukata*, and lifted his saké cup to his mouth.

"The forgeries probably sold better."

"I suppose so. The name *Tekishintei* would certainly sell better than the name *Kankotei*."

"On the whole, what kind of man was he? Do you remember him?" As I was beginning to feel more or less curious about this counterfeiter, I also wanted to know about his personal appearance.

"I really don't remember anything about that. It was when I was very little. Besides, you see, I only caught glimpses of him in the hallway or places like that. One time though, oh yes, it happened about the time my father was around forty and I guess I was seven or eight . . ." and from out of the recesses of his memory Takuhiko related what was left of his deepest impressions of that time.

He did not clearly or wholly recollect where the place was, but apparently it was at some exhibition. Hosen was on his knees on the floor, with his head lowered, and Keigaku was standing in front of him, saying: "Lift your head up and look at me."

As Takuhiko vaguely recalled, there had been some shouting about something. Keigaku had gotten violently excited and kept on shouting, repeating the same thing over and over, while Hosen at that time merely kept his eyes lowered without saying a word. Takuhiko was left with absolutely no impression about the personal appearance of Hosen at that time, but, he said, in his childish heart he had had a tremendous feeling of compassion for the man.

"It was because my father had that kind of temperament, I think. On discovering that there were forgeries, he shouted abuses in front of people without compunction, you know what I mean? We weren't at home, so I guess that he was caught by my father at one of my father's exhibitions, at a department store, museum, temple, or someplace like that. Even so, I think my father may have given him some money after that. So, this has gotten to be a kind of apocryphal story."

Takuhiko smiled. Actually, however, it appears that Keigaku was quite charitable toward Hosen and gave him money more than once or twice. Takuhiko also had recollections of hearing things like that from his mother or from Keigaku. He had vague memories of two other occasions when he had met a man who resembled Hosen. There was something about Hosen's being summoned and rebuked or coming to borrow money. In any case, he always got the same feeling he had had on that occasion when he had caught a flashing glimpse of the man who would not lift his head up.

"In all likelihood, that time when he sat on the floor and couldn't lift his eyes may have been the last time that he appeared before my father. After getting to be of junior high school age, I never heard of Hosen's coming to visit my father. But my father used to say in retrospect that he had a good-for-nothing rascal for a friend."

That night we sat in front of Hosen Hara's painting, drinking saké until very late and made up our beds in front of that picture.

III

THE SECOND time I ran into the name of Hosen Hara was a year and a half after I had traveled to the towns and villages of the Inland Sea coast with Takuhiko Onuki. I know that because it was the year the war ended, the spring of 1945. During that year and a half, the course of the war had taken a drastic turn for the worse. At home, the people's lives and spirits—and even Nature—were rough and ruined beyond recognition. With the help of an acquaintance of mine, a colleague at the newspaper where I worked, I was having my mother, my frail wife, and my two infant children evacuated to a mountain village, a place near the summit of the Chugoku mountain range. It was a spot near the juncture of three prefectures, Okayama, Tottori, and Hiroshima. It was a tiny place, literally a mountain nook near the border of Tottori Prefecture. It was a place where one had the feeling that here, and here alone, night and day would peacefully follow each other with no change from the old days, no matter what the result of the war.

It was the end of March when I first set out to preview the place where my family would be evacuated. I knew of only one man to whom I could turn in that village. His name was Senzo Onoe, and he was an acquaintance of my colleague at the newspaper. The five-mile road leading from the mountain-top station on the Harima-Bizen line to this place is, as might be expected, a steep mountain path which one person can barely traverse. Along the way, it is necessary to go over two small but sharp ridges, but on entering the hamlet, one finds a remarkably flat area, a tableland, and the prospect opens and extends easily from here in all four directions. The rays of the sun and the fragrance in the wind are different from what they are anywhere else in the world.

34

There are some fifty houses scattered over that broad tableland, and the whole village is filled with a shadeless brilliance, even though this sometimes only imparts a feeling of emptiness. I first experienced the real sensation of "sunbeams descending" when I came to this highland. A shallow river only thirty feet wide, whose upstream and downstream are indistinguishable, turns and flows north at that place.

Escorted by Senzo Onoe, who was wearing the kind of farmer's field smock that we Japanese call *noragi*, I was shown a place in the hamlet that might be leased— the Youth Assembly Hall. Although it was called that, it was a structure in a style that was hardly different from that of the ordinary village houses. I immediately decided to rent it for evacuating my family. Then, that night I stayed at Onoe's house. The villagers were the kind of relatively large-scale farmers that are not seen in other places. At every house, two or three oxen were kept, and even in the construction of their homes, the villagers retained a rough, old-fashioned atmosphere. Onoe's family was the oldest in the community, and compared with the other houses, his was a size larger. I was invited to sleep in the guest room, which was separated from the storeroom by a partition of one large panel of cypress.

In the curiously small, half-sized *tokonoma* of this guest room, I saw something that excited me. It was Keigaku Onuki's picture of a fox under a peony bush with his head turned facing outward. I uttered an exclamation of surprise. It was not appropriate for a mountaineer farmer to have a masterpiece like this in his *tokonoma*, no matter how prosperous he might be.

Gesturing toward the picture, I said to the fifty-year-old owner of the house, who could not possibly be interested in such art, "That's a superb thing, isn't it?"

"It wasn't an easy thing to come by for people like us,

I understand," said Onoe. For some unknown reason, he showed a shyness in his sun-blackened, rough, but honest-looking face. "Really," he went on, "a man who said he was a bosom friend of this Keigaku who painted it was in this village, and . . ."

"What was the man called?" I asked.

"His name was Hosen Hara. He was a painter, too. Some years back—when was it? 1940, I think—he died. He originally came from these parts and came back here in his later years."

Even without asking for an explanation, I understood the rest. It was a surprise to me that Hosen Hara came from this place. But as soon as I heard that he had died, even though he was a complete stranger to me, I felt a certain deep emotion for a while. Two years after Keigaku had passed away, his counterfeiter, Hosen Hara, had followed him to the next world!

That night I informed Takuhiko Onuki in Kyoto that the counterfeiter Hosen Hara had died and that I was evacuating my family to Hara's birthplace. In my letter to Takuhiko, who probably was himself feverishly engaged in evacuating the massive art works that Keigaku had bequeathed, I wrote about the incredible thing that had happened.

Evacuating my family to this village took a month, and the purple *akebia* flowers were already blooming in the thicket behind the Youth Assembly Hall where the four helpless members of my family were to live from then on. It was the end of April, but the temperature was still low, and when you put your hand into the small river in front of the house, the water was as cold as in winter.

After the five days it took me to get my family fairly well settled, I went back to Osaka. Before that, I went to call at the home of the village headman, whose family standing was second only to Onoe's. And there I was disturbed to find in his guest room a second Keigaku forgery painted by Hosen Hara. It was a counterfeit of the painting "Flowers and Birds," over a foot and three-quarters wide, an imposing thing to look at.

To Onoe and the village headman I of course said nothing about the secret of these works. At a time when, throughout Japan, life and death themselves were so uncertain, I didn't have the heart to impose any needless worries upon the people who thought that these were Keigaku's work. The counterfeited Keigakus painted by Hosen Hara undoubtedly would not in all eternity go out of this hamlet on the mountain summit. For hundreds and thousands of years, I reflected, they would be passed on to people who didn't even know the name of Keigaku Onuki. In all likelihood, no matter what happened to Japan, this fact would not change. As these thoughts flashed through my mind, I felt that I was witnessing Eternity. It also seems to me that during this period my anxiety about entrusting my family to the customs and manners of an unknown and unfamiliar place was over-riding the concern for forgeries I had had about a year and a half earlier.

From then until August when the war ended, I went to that village three times to see my family. I believe it was on that third occasion that I went on behalf of another colleague of mine to look at still another vacant house in this hamlet, escorted this time by an old bent-over farmer-woman who was acting as the agent. The house was on the slope of a short hill which rose lazily south of the hamlet, and it could be said to be the highest house in the village. There it stood removed from the center of the population. There, as I learned from the prattle of the old woman who was guiding me, was the house in which Hosen Hara had lived. Although it was almost five years since Hosen had died, that house was still vacant and just as he had left it.

The house was in complete disorder. It was not originally Hosen's house, but he had returned to this village the year that the Manchurian Incident broke out and had "bought it for a song." She went on to say things to the effect that Hosen had left his own small hamlet, which was actually about two miles away, because he did not get along with his older brother and that because of their relationship, when he returned to his native place, he had taken this house instead of going back to the hamlet where he had been raised.

"How about his family?" I asked the old woman, thinking it strange that the house had been left empty after his death.

"You mean his wife? She ran away." The old woman said this as though it were nothing at all.

"Ran away?"

"She probably got mad at him. She lived with Uncle Hosen in this house for three years. Then, at the time of a festival, she went home to her family in Shoyama and stayed there and never came back."

Hosen had even gone to beg her to come back. And also a man in the neighborhood, worried about them, had acted as a go-between, but in the end she had not come back. Hosen, for some reason unknown to the old woman, had been adopted into his wife's family and had taken their name, Hara, so unless he chose to withdraw that name from the registry, there could be no divorce. Her family was indifferent to all this, but in any case, the two had separated.

"When the old man died, I guess his wife did come. At least she may have come at the time of the funeral, but until then she didn't come back even once."

"About how old a person is she?"

"When he died, the old man was sixty-seven or eight.

She was about ten years younger, so she must be past sixty now. I hear that she's being supported by her relatives in Shoyama," said the old woman.

So, in his declining years, Hosen had returned to his native village a wrecked counterfeiter and had died in the village where he was born, but even those last years, as related by the old woman, were punctuated with shadows of misfortune.

Still wearing my *zori*, I entered the dilapidated vacant house. For no particular reason, I opened a cupboard near the hearth and looked in. The interior was packed full of all kinds of trash covered with dust and cobwebs. Poking her head in beside mine and removing some plates from inside the cupboard, the old woman said something to the effect that they could still be used.

Then, she shook the dust off them and put them on the threshold, intending to take them back with her later.

"These are things Uncle Hosen used when he was making fireworks."

"Fireworks?"

"He used to make fireworks here."

Then, muttering that all of these things were paraphernalia for making fireworks, she raked the rubbish out of the cupboard with her cane, and it came tumbling down on the worn-out *tatami*. A black powdery substance, mixed with dust, whirled around over the floor, blown by the breeze.

"He said it was gunpowder, so everybody's been afraid to sweep it away." As she said this, the old woman without a speck of concern raked the stuff all over the *tatami*. Three or four round things, like halves of India rubber balls, came bouncing out. Since of course these things too had formerly contained gunpowder, a little bit of yellow-colored powder still adhered to the bottom of them. Things that looked like they might have been round papier-mâché cases for fireworks, paper sacks with their sides split and black powder oozing out of their insides, some pellet-shaped articles of unknown character, solidifiers that might be for refining the black powder, dishes for mixing paint, writing brushes, spatulas, painting brushes, a sheaf of Japanese paper, mortars—all sorts of things like that were scattered around in there.

I was somewhat surprised to hear that Hosen Hara had been making fireworks. We stepped down into the *doma*.* The *doma* had all kinds of trash and chaff scattered over it, just like the cupboard, but to such an extent that there was hardly room to set one's foot down. The chaff, the old woman explained, was something Hosen used inside of sky rockets.

"The old man used to sit over there and make the fireworks."

I looked at the place she was indicating. It was a shaded place just beyond the *doma* which might have been a little barn at any other farmhouse. She pointed out what was undoubtedly his former workshop. A wooden bench and a tree stump on which he used to sit amidst the disorderly trash confirmed this. Set on the sill of a small window, which was the only place through which the sunlight entered, were a half-broken measuring device and a number of chemical bottles. Slips of paper with prayers invoking protection from fire were pasted on the lintels between the doors and ceiling. Cleaning this house and putting it into the kind of shape that would enable a person to live in it was going to be far from easy. The moment I set foot in this house, I rejected it as a home to which my friend could evacuate.

* In pre-modern Japanese architecture, the *doma* was an unfloored multi-purpose area, set lower than the rest of the house and used as a storage area, as a pantry, and as the kitchen. Separate kitchens have only recently begun to replace the *doma* in urban areas; in rural areas, the *doma* persists.

Standing in the middle of this *doma,* where disorder was really carried to extremes, I surveyed this dingy corner that she had called a fireworks factory. I couldn't imagine what sort of appearance or mien the strange dead Hosen Hara had possessed, but the image that first drifted into my mind at that moment was one of some sort of shriveling, sluggish animal crouching in that dark spot. Could it have been because he used to sit on that tree stump in front of that wooden bench, fingering black or red or yellow powders in that measuring device? The sunbeams would be floating in, creating bands of light behind him, but the atmosphere surrounding those sun-rays would be stagnant, dark, and cold. Certainly, that was the picture I had of Hosen Hara in this dark and wretched house, forever beyond redemption—a much more miserable picture than I ever had of Hosen Hara, the counterfeiter.

"There's something about this I don't like," I thought. And the moment I thought this, I recalled the marvelous spirit that had pervaded the *sumie* painting by Hosen that Takuhiko Onuki and I had chanced upon at the inn in Himeji. I had the feeling that something closely resembling what was latent in that *sumie* painting filled this eerie, deserted house, but this time in a much more foul and filthy form.

As we were leaving, we went around to the back of the house. It was then that the old woman showed me Hara's grave. Behind the house was a small vacant lot which ended in a six-foot drop. Near the edge of the drop, a nondescript, ordinary stone—Hosen's tombstone—was set half-buried in the weeds. Out beyond that small tombstone loomed the prospect. In the distance you could see the numerous ridges of the mountain range, one upon the other, rolling in gentle slopes, and closer, as you dropped your eyes, the separate village houses studded the flats, looking in their smallness like toys, luxuriant

41

with the many surrounding trees. It was April, but this was not a spring landscape. The whole landscape seemed submerged as though it were an underwater scene —and cold.

That night, I heard from the usually extremely poor conversationalist, Senzo Onoe, a somewhat detailed story about Hosen Hara's declining years in this hamlet.

According to that story, Hosen Hara and his wife Asa came back to this hamlet the year the Manchurian Incident broke out, in a condition that could almost literally be called "with only the clothes they had on their backs." They hadn't brought a single piece of baggage that could really be called baggage, but on the other hand, they apparently had a certain amount of money. They had bought the House on the Heights, as it was called in the village, which had become vacant when the preceding occupants had all died of consumption one after another. They had gotten the house for a song—but that was the asking price—had immediately paid cash for it, and moved in.

It was soon after moving to this village that Hosen began to palm off those works that the village headman, Onoe, and one or two other families in the village claimed were Keigaku scrolls. Before he was twenty, when he had left the village, Hosen had said he would become an artist, but since he had really only returned once or twice until his later years, there was almost no one in the village who knew anything in detail about his character. At one point, a long time ago, there had been rumors in circulation in the village that Hosen had become a successful painter in the Kyoto-Osaka area. Because of this, whenever the villagers mentioned him in their conversations, there was something in their stories that indicated that they casually regarded Hosen as a person who had left the village and succeeded in the city. Accordingly, the villagers were a bit surprised at the wretched condition he was in when he came back home in his later years. Hosen told them then that he had come back to the country because in recent years his right shoulder had been so wracked with pain from rheumatism that he could not wield his paintbrushes and delicate work was impossible and that, in addition, his savings had run out.

When he had settled down in the village, he didn't do any kind of work in particular, but from time to time he could be seen taking his scrolls and curios to Yonago, Okayama, Tottori, and other places and bringing different things back. At any rate, he seemed to be eking out a living carrying on some sort of art business in the countryside.

Hosen had left a fairly good impression on the villagers, and there wasn't any particular single instance of his doing anything to cause trouble for other people. People would call him "Hosen-san, Hosen-san," with more or less mixed feelings of respect and affection. But after a while, as time went on, he started to go to other places less and less frequently; rumors began to circulate to the effect that he was tinkering with gunpowder—actually he was making firecrackers and fireworks and selling them to the toy stores in Yonago—and at some point he gradually came to be called simply "Uncle Hosen" by the villagers.

Of course, even though he was engaged in making fireworks, it was illegal. It would seem that even when he first moved into the village he had already been working with gunpowder. Once, late at night, Onoe said, balls of fire were flying directly over Uncle Hosen's house, and the villagers became greatly agitated. Later, when they learned that these things were sky rockets that he had shot off, they were very shocked.

In the third year after Hosen moved to this village, he exploded some gunpowder and lost three fingers from his right hand. After that accident occurred, a resentment developed among the villagers toward the repugnant things that he had been tinkering with, and Hosen rather abruptly lost his popularity with them. Curiously though, after he had had the accident, Hosen turned cocky, and from then on he produced half-publicly the fireworks that he had been turning out furtively until then.

The villagers did not go near Hosen's house very often, but on the rare occasions when they did try poking around his house, they would find him in the workshop he had converted from a barn or see him sitting there constantly making all sorts of toy fireworks, apparently on order for Yonago.

It was just half a year after Hosen lost his fingers that he and his wife Asa separated. At that time, even though she had deserted him, Senzo Onoe acted as a go-between and went to Asa's family home at Shoyama to appeal to her to come back to Hosen. But Asa simply and persistently just kept saying, "*I won't do it!*" Neighbors one after another also went up to Shoyama two or three times, but it was useless. At length, Hosen said that if he was such a despicable person, he, for his part, would abandon the idea of reconciliation with Asa—and that would be that. The villagers furthermore did not particularly condemn Asa for leaving the husband to whom she had been married for such a long time. Minus the three fingers, Hosen's right hand was quite unsightly, and as he tinkered with gunpowder in his dismal workshop, he had a gloominess that would cause anyone to despise him, even a wife.

He could not produce the fireworks publicly because it was of course against the law. He nevertheless continued to turn them out and apparently became fairly well off. It seems that he regularly donated money for the construction of the town roads and made sizeable monetary contributions to the neighborhood functions with donations that appreciably exceeded what was expected. Once—Onoe didn't know when it was—a policeman came around and hauled Hosen off to the police station in a neighboring town, but somehow he was acquitted and did not have to pay a fine. Even after that, Hosen continued to make his living the same way as before, still in his dark and gloomy workshop.

At any rate, the fact is that before he died in 1940, Hosen spent almost ten years of his lonely life in this hamlet. For about the last three years, however, because he had made a small fortune, the villagers rarely saw him produce fireworks. Usually, he was just on the porch, sometimes just sitting there, sometimes sleeping, mostly just doing nothing but gazing abstractedly ahead. Still, in the summer, when he was asked to do so by the neighborhood youths, he would make a few fireworks and accept the small gratuities they offered him. Moreover, if he was badgered into it, he would wrap up some of the fireworks he had made and go himself to shoot them off in the neighboring villages at the summer festivals. As a result, it appears that he was regarded more affectionately as "Uncle Hosen" by the people in other villages than by those in this one.

Hosen's death came suddenly. Early one morning when the autumn rain had been pouring down continuously, his next door neighbor, who actually lived a full block away, became curious about the fact that "Uncle Hosen" had not shown up for two or three days, so he went over to visit him. Hosen was lying on his face in the *doma,* dead. When the neighbor tried touching him, it was obvious from the rigidity and coldness of the dead body that many hours had passed since his death. The cause of Hosen Hara's death was apoplexy.

An interesting thing in connection with Hosen's passing away was that just prior to his death he apparently had been intending to work with his paint-brushes. This could be deduced from the fact that in the storeroom there was a blanket, folded in two, on top of which a number of dishes for mixing paint had been arranged in order. Beside them, five paintbrushes had been placed with their necks neatly lined up on the cover of an inkstone case. Right in the middle of the blanket, a sheet of brand new white paper on which nothing had been painted was spread out just as neatly. It was thought that he had been just intending to take up his brush when he remembered something he had to attend to, had stepped down into the *doma*, and had passed away there just like that.

"Was Hosen-san painting pictures in his later years?" I asked Senzo Onoe.

"I don't think he was painting any more. But he was a painter at heart, so I guess it must have been on his mind, even when he had a hunch that he was going to die. Some people might say that he was going to paint, but he was missing three fingers, so it wouldn't have been easy to paint anything worth mentioning," he replied.

That was the last of the counterfeiter, but there was something in that story that struck me. Onoe had said that drawing paper without a single brush stroke on it had been spread out and ready, but I had the feeling that he really had no intention of painting a picture at that time. I felt rather that he only wanted to surround himself with his painting gear.

I listened to this tale of Hosen Hara to the end, and when I got up to leave, Senzo Onoe said, as though he had suddenly remembered something, "By the way, inside a cabinet in the storeroom of your house there are some things Uncle Hosen wrote. I think there's some-thing he wrote about fireworks. Those things were found at the time of his funeral, and some of the young boys must have thought they might be of use some day and stored them in the Assembly Hall."

There was one cabinet in the storeroom of the house I had rented which we had not touched and had left alone as promised when I had leased the house. I didn't know what was in it but had guessed that it must contain things that were owned jointly by the young people of the village.

On returning home, I opened that cabinet. An account book of festival receipts, minutes of a youth conference, drafts of speeches—trash of that sort was crammed into it. In among these things, I discovered a notebook of bound Japanese rice-paper with the words *Outline of Procedures Governing the Manufacture of Pyrotechnics* skillfully written, by brush of course, on the cover. The title was pretentious, but these things appeared to be something like memoranda which Hosen Hara had written himself on the making of fireworks. When I opened up the notebook and looked at a page, there was a heading, "Fog Blooms; Red Fog; Snowfall," with this formula underneath:

"In order to make stars, prepare a saffron core and set it aside to dry; then add clay to chrysanthemum powder,* mix with water, add $1\frac{1}{2}\%$ magnesium, and stir in a mortar; wrap the resulting paste around the core in layers; after the core is well covered with the paste, sprinkle with a mixture made from 15 oz. of chrysanthemum and $1\frac{1}{2}$ oz. of seed.** Roll the ball well and repeat this process several times. When it gets to be four

* I am informed by makers of Japanese fireworks that "chrysanthemum powder" is a technical term for a mixture of charcoal, sulphur, and potassium nitrate in proportions that will produce a chrysanthemum-shaped flare when exploded in the air.
** Seeds and chaff were used as retarding catalysts until sawdust replaced them due to regulations in some countries against the import of agricultural products.

or five inches, add a booster. Be sure to dry the ball in the sun after each application. Cores of 5¾ inches and 7½ inches can be used."

Very unclear passages like this covered three pages. Then followed paragraphs on combinations of saffron and combinations of chrysanthemum. Proportions for each kind of explosive were written by brush in red. Then followed sections on the manufacture of "Roman Candles," "Floral Cores," "Firetails," etc. Of course these were Hosen's memoranda to himself, but to me, who had absolutely no knowledge of fireworks, they were completely incomprehensible. There was a sheet of Japanese rice-paper stuffed between one set of inter-leaves. I opened it and looked at it. It was Hosen's own *curriculum vitae,* a personal statement of interest to me for very special reasons.

"Born: October 3, 1874; Senjiro (pen-name: Hosen) Hara," was written at the beginning, so there was no question that this was Hosen's own *curriculum vitae.* However, his record of employment, which can only be regarded as fictitious, was listed simply in this sketchy fashion:

"1916, Arareya Fireworks Store, Tokyo

1918, Suzuki Fireworks Store, Yokosuka

1921, In Charge of the Oriental Pyrotechnical Factory

1922, Sakai Fireworks Display Store, Osaka

1924, In Charge of the Marudama Pyrotechnics Factory, Osaka"

At the end, there was an ostentatious subscript: *"The foregoing is certified as factual."*

It is not clear where, when, or to whom he intended to submit this. This much, however, is clear: the period from 1912 to 1926 was precisely the time he was dispensing Keigaku forgeries as he moved around in the small cities and towns of Hyogo and Okayama Prefectures. It is therefore also clear that this was a wholly fabricated statement of his personal history. The possibility exists that when Hosen reached an impasse trying to earn a living as a counterfeiter or as a village artist, he might have been a technician in charge of a fireworks factory at one or another country town—on the side. If you want to stretch your imagination even further, you could even say that when he was ordered to appear at the police station, he was possibly able to settle the matter very quickly by just producing this false document and wrapping the police up in smoke. In any case, there is no doubt that this document clearly reveals a characteristic part of the nature of the person that was Hosen Hara.

IV

"I DON'T know whether you know it or not, but making fireworks in the winter can be very unpleasant. Chilean nitrate can be awfully cold when it's cold." As she said this, Hosen Hara's widow looked at the palm of her right hand as if she were recalling the chapped hands she had in those days. Then she dropped her gaze.

My talk with her took place at the end of November, the year the war ended.

Although the war had ended, life in the city was still shrouded in great post-war confusion and anxiety, and almost every day newspaper articles were reporting on the gangs of robbers, so I kept my family at their evacuation site where they were. I had intended in any case to have them spend the rest of the year there. The seasons changed in that mountain village as much as a month earlier than in other places, and toward the end of September, piercing blasts from the bleak and dismal autumn winds came whistling incessantly up the slopes of the mountain range, producing terrific drafts which blew all the way from Mimasaku to Hoki. At the beginning of October, the continual late-autumnal rains that are characteristic of the highlands arrived as the first harbingers of winter.

As that time approached, my wife seemed to develop a feeling of panic over spending the winter snowbound in an unfamiliar place. When I went to visit her there at the beginning of October, she suddenly broke the news to me that she wanted to move out of this place of refuge, and the sooner the better. After I returned to Osaka, my wife urged me persistently in letter after letter to move them out of their evacuation place. She lacked the self-confidence, she wrote, to spend the winter here . . . surrounded by an old woman and two infants . . . and without heating equipment . . . and if the children caught pneumonia, there wasn't a doctor, and . . .!

About the middle of November, I took a fairly long leave of absence from my company and left for that hamlet in the highlands of Tottori Prefecture in order to move my family. There I encountered a whole series of various and sundry impediments to getting things like transportation and shipment of effects taken care of. By the time I had taken the last step and managed to arrange some means for shipping our effects and transporting the family, November was almost over.

On the last afternoon, in order to arrange for the shipment of our baggage via the San-in Line, I set out for the station at Shoyama, a place whose name I had so often heard but which I had never visited. If I could have sent our things from the neighboring mountain-top station, which I always used and where I knew the station master, I would have had no problem. But those two steep ridges on the mountain road leading to our house were a formidable obstacle.

Negotiations over the baggage at Shoyama station were settled much more simply than I had expected. According to the conversation I had with the station personnel, if I waited until evening, a truck could be sent from there to the hamlet where I lived. So, since I thought that I might just as well save myself the trouble of walking that five-mile mountain road again, I decided to go back with the truck when they sent it.

As I was wondering how I might best kill the two hours until the truck left, I suddenly remembered hearing that Hosen Hara's widow was living here supported by her elder brother. I tried to think of some particular reason why I had to visit Hosen Hara's widow, but I couldn't come up with one. I did eventually come up with an idea. Rather than approach her to talk about Hosen or anything connected with him, I would ask her instead about anecdotes or anything else I might not yet have heard concerning Keigaku Onuki, whose biography I had to write. With this excuse in mind, I got up the courage to go and visit her.

I asked about Hosen Hara's wife at the general store in front of the station and got an immediate answer. I was told that until two or three years ago Asa had run a little store selling cheap sweets in front of the station, but as the intensity of the war increased and the things she sold became so scarce, she had to close the store. They didn't know what she was doing now, but she was being supported by her elder brother who had a lumber yard or something. I met Asa at the porch of this house, which, while it could not be considered luxurious, was a well-built and excellent house.

I was unable to tell, of course, whether she was happy or unhappy living with her elder brother. She had a trim figure, and as the late afternoon sun fell on her there on the narrow porch, she was peeling persimmons with a kitchen knife getting them ready to dry. The young proprietor of the saké distillery in Wake had told us that she was of small stature and beautiful. And indeed she must have been beautiful when she was young. Even as a woman of sixty, there was still left in her that chicness in both appearance and expression that is usually met in entertainment people. But when she showed her profile, her earlobes were shallow, and here and there, there were traces of tragedy and an air of extreme poverty. I had thought that she would have an aversion to talking about Hosen because he had spent his life dishonestly as a painter, but she showed no such tendency whatsoever.

"It might *look* as if he had some close association with Keigaku-*sensei* when he was young, and after I married him he may have gone up to Kyoto on occasion and visited the *sensei's* home at Hyakumamben. But he did not have any connection that could really be called a *close* association. Anyhow, the fact is that he counterfeited the *sensei's* works inordinately, and so he couldn't show himself in front of Keigaku-*sensei*."

It was surprising, the degree to which this woman had disassociated herself from Hosen. She gave me the impression that as far as she was concerned all the bad acts of this man to whom she had been married for so long were already past, gone, and forgotten, and she had no connection with them.

"I separated from that man in 1935. From then until the time he died, he only came to visit me once. That was on the day the newspapers announced Keigaku-*sensei's* death."

Asa told me that on that day when Hosen came to visit her he had said something like, "Why won't you substitute for me and go and burn some incense at Keigaku's altar instead of me, because I can't hold my head up even at his funeral." Asa told me that she had wondered at the time why, instead of feeling the need to go and apologize for the great trouble he had caused Keigaku, he had acted as though a sadness over the death of an old friend was gripping him.

"No matter what anyone else says, I believe that his spirit was broken after coming to these mountains. Even though he had no reason for it, he held a grudge against Keigaku-*sensei* until then. When he used to drink, he would say that if *he* wanted to paint, *he* could paint pictures as well as the other fellow; when he was young, *he* was the more skillful of the two; *he* also had talent. But, after coming to these mountains, when mentioning Keigaku, he would sometimes say, 'It's such a great thing that he's so famous.' "

That was Asa's story. And the image that then drifted into my mind of Hosen who after reading the news of Keigaku's death had come up to this hamlet to visit the wife who had deserted him, the image of him moving along the winding, hilly road which I myself had just that very day walked, that image curiously crystallized as one of a little person together with the late autumn winds crossing the marvelous bamboo thickets that filled the slopes of the mountain range. However, thinking about it later, I recalled that the anniversary date of Keigaku's death was March third. So, it would have been a time when one side of these mountains was still covered with snow, and Hosen might have been wearing straw snowshoes and trudging stolidly across the snow packed mountain road to get to Shoyama. And *even then,* apparently, Asa had not gone to Keigaku's funeral in Kyoto, and that's the way the matter stood.

In any event, the fact that there was a day such as that in Hosen's declining years suddenly struck me like a ray of sunlight amidst the generally dark and dismal colorless monotone of this person called Hosen who was inexplicably commanding my attention.

Asa's talk about Keigaku ended, I asked her obliquely,

though I myself thought it was rude, why she had decided to separate from Hosen. Soon after Hosen came to the mountains and started to manufacture fireworks, she began to want to leave him for doing that kind of work. She herself sometimes had to assist him—"Oh, well, it was making a living, if you can call it a living, so what could I do?"—but apparently she hated Hosen for engaging in that work even more she hated the job itself.

"Even when that man began to counterfeit Keigaku-*sensei's* work, he sneakingly kept it a secret from me. It finally came out in the open, but at first, as you might expect, just my knowing it seemed an embarrassment to him. He carried on these activities as secretly as he could so that I wouldn't know about them. And when he started making fireworks, it was just the same. This time it was not that he was doing anything particularly bad, although there are laws about amateurs handling explosives. It was just that he hid things from me, no matter what he did. If he had only been open about it, everything might have been all right. But when I wasn't there or after I'd gone to bed, he used to sneak over to the edge of the porch and stealthily grind things in his mortar. It was because he did that sort of thing that I got to dislike fireworks."

What apparently first motivated Hosen to tinker with explosives was that there was someone he liked, the owner of a curio store, who made fireworks, and during the time he was associated with that person, he himself developed an interest in making fireworks. When Asa first became aware of it, Hosen was furtively wrapping all sorts of chemicals in paper in roughly equal quantities of about an ounce-and-a-half each and igniting them to see what color their flames would be.

"Why in the world did he find fireworks so interesting?"

"Well," replied Asa a bit pensively, "he was a funny man. I don't know where he ever got the idea, but once he was trying to produce a certain deep blue-violet color and he acted as though he was obsessed. He generally could get that color by mixing Paris green with chlorate of potash and pine resin, but he seemed to be trying to find some means for producing a chrysanthemum of this deep bluish violet—it was supposed to be the color of bell-flowers—but it always ended up a little pale and different from the original bell-flower color."

Hosen lost three of his fingers when he was making shooting stars. He had incorrectly inserted a fuse in the side of an explosive he had been devising, and it accidentally ignited, the explosives nearby catching fire in the process. It was quite a serious thing. Although Asa was quite upset by the incident itself, it additionally provided her with an excuse for leaving him—and she made up her mind to do so. Ever since he had begun working secretly with explosives, she said, she had developed a strong dislike for Hosen, and her dislike had continued. When the explosion accident occurred, it was the last straw, and she really wanted to leave him for good.

"Did he ever achieve that blue-violet?" I asked.

"Mm-m, I wonder. He apparently was not very satisfied with it while I was still with him," she replied but acted as though she really had little interest in that subject. While she was relating stories about Hosen, some of the earlier love and affection she had felt toward him, even though he was such a strange person, had more or less been revived, and even though she now displayed an attitude of cold indifference and detachment, she certainly did not say anything bad about him intentionally.

"In the final analysis, he was an unfortunate man, that man, don't you think? I really think so. It may look as though I wasted my whole life on account of him, but I sometimes wonder if he wasn't even more unhappy than I was. It was his curse to care more about painting pictures than about his three meals a day; in the long run, he got started on the wrong track and ended up without painting a single worthwhile picture; when he made fireworks, he lost three fingers; he was almost driven to distraction over 'deep purple, deep purple'— but he couldn't even produce that! He wasn't a particularly bad man, but I guess he was just born unlucky."

For over an hour I listened to Asa's tales. While listening to her stories, I was captivated by the way she talked about this person Hosen as she stared fixedly into the distance and by the way she was in certain respects still bound up with him.

It was my observation that during the course of almost thirty years that she had lived with him during their marriage, she had been an individual unto herself and had developed a special kind of mentality not generally found in women.

"Do you know the proprietor of the big saké distillery in Wake?" I asked, recalling the owner's statement that Hosen and she had frequently visted his home.

"No, I don't," she answered promptly, as if the distillery was something completely unknown to her. Perhaps my reference to something in her younger days had displeased her. The thought also suddenly occurred to me that the person who used to frequent that house with him might have been some other woman, so I dropped the subject.

At that point, without even having a cup of tea, I cut short my curious visit with this stranger from whom I had heard things that really infringed on her privacy, and I left so as not to be late for my five-o'clock truck.

Of all the things I had heard from Hosen's widow that day, the story about Hosen trying to shoot off the blue-violet chrysanthemum interested me most. At the time that I heard it, it didn't even seem particularly important, but it curiously remained in my mind, cropping up unexpectedly from time to time.

After we moved out of our evacuation site and were living in an Osaka suburb, I casually disclosed to my wife the desire—or, to overstate the case, the dream—that Hosen had cherished in his declining years. As soon as she heard it, she winced and spontaneously exclaimed, "Awful!"

"Why 'awful!'?"

"Because. I can't really explain it, but for some reason it gave me an unpleasant feeling—ghastly! A deep-violet flare opening against the black sky! That was probably what made me feel so queasy."

Then, I too was struck by the thought that I was dabbling in something I should not touch. With that, I hurriedly dropped the story of Hosen I had intended to tell. That is all there was to it and it had no particular significance, but my wife's attitude of that moment has remained fixedly in my mind as a totally unexpected and revealing discovery. I believe I generally understand my wife's feelings, but even when I probed this thing in depth, there was something incomprehensible, or at least I couldn't understand it. I could believe that there was something discernible in Hosen that could have caused my wife to feel something intolerably unpleasant just as it caused his wife to leave him. Although she had managed to go tagging along after him through a life of several decades of counterfeiting, there must have been something—something incomprehensible to people like me—something deep-rooted in the physical revulsion she felt, so that she as a woman could not trail after the Hosen who produced explosives.

Hosen's production of fireworks, the gunpowder, and the chemicals he used, these cold and dismal things somehow engendered the same feelings even in me. I could not, however, feel this in the same way my wife and Hosen's widow might have felt it. I could catch at least a fleeting glimpse of the piteous beauty which a multi-petaled bell-flower color bursting open for an instant in the night sky might have meant to this one counterfeiter whose life had been wrecked and who possessed nothing. However, I still wondered if this dream of Hosen Hara had really ever opened up in the sky at night. There was no way of asking the deceased man and confirming that it had. But certainly, had it on the other hand *not* been the color of petals opening, wouldn't the two women have winced anyhow and wouldn't they have reacted just as tempestuously?

That was the line of my thought.

V

AFTER that, the case of Hosen Hara gradually disappeared from my mind without my realizing it. As time went by, the not-too-cheerful story of this dead counterfeiter whom I had learned about accidentally and through hearsay from people at our evacuation site would, in the course of events, rather naturally become dim in my memory. Two years after the war, however, Hosen was once again brought before my mind's eye as though it were a finale to the stories I had heard about him.

It was summer. At that time, I was all involved and wrapped up in problems of provincial culture. For the first time in a year and several months, I took a train on the Harima-Bizen Line which crosses over to Yonago from Okayama Prefecture. I was on my way to cover a general art exhibition at one of the San-In Prefectures around the Japan Sea in order to do an article for the Sunday supplements.

58

As the train pulled up to the platforms at the small mountain-top stations where I had gotten on and off so often loaded down with supplies on my back, I gazed out at the stalks of the tall growing weeds swaying in the highland winds and at the red-soil banks on the west side of the station; and always there was the sound of pebbles rolling down the banks to the road below. Suddenly it occurred to me that it would be no great loss if I arrived at my destination one train later. I vacillated for a while over whether to get off or not, but just as the train was on the verge of departing, I grabbed my valise from the string-net shelf and hopped off the train.

This place was filled with a thousand and one bitter-sweet memories of things not experienced elsewhere due to the times. Even though I did not go to the hamlet which had been my family's refuge, I still thought it would not be a bad idea to spend up to two hours in the station square looking up at the familiar landscape and the rows of houses in the hamlet. If I did not seize this opportunity to get off and wander around this station, I might not get a second chance. Possibly I might meet some of the villagers I knew, even if I only knew them by sight. Thinking these thoughts, I went through the gate and headed for the only restaurant there was in the square, intending to relax there. As I proceeded to walk toward the restaurant, I was brought to a halt on hearing from somewhere behind me in the character-istic local dialect: "Aren't you the fellow from the As-sembly Hall?"

I turned around. It was the second son of the farmer who lived next door to the elementary school, a family affectionately and jokingly called the "People-Out-Back." He was the young man who always helped us with the firewood.

I stood there and chatted with him. The boy talked

about the difficult times the farmers were having, in terms that indicated a rather pinkish political attitude. He didn't ask for news about my family, nor did he even mention any of the residents of the hamlet. Anger over our difficult times, for reasons he didn't understand, was building a fire in the head of this young highlander.

"You going into the village?" he asked.

I explained that I did not have the time so I couldn't go today, but I asked him to take my best wishes and greetings to everyone. The youth then informed me that starting at sundown, for the first time since the war, there was to be a fireworks display in which five towns were jointly participating; that in just two hours crowds of people would be assembling for this spectacle; that among them would be people from our hamlet; that it would not take long—so why didn't I wait around for it? I had intended to be one train late anyhow, so I decided to make it two. I reasoned that if I met some of the villagers here, I could fulfill some of my obligations by thanking all these people for their many courtesies during the time of our evacuation.

It was now three o'clock. I spent the next two hours in the station waiting room and at the restaurant. On the telephone poles in the station square exceedingly crude and clumsy handbills had been posted. They were written with smudged red ink, probably by the young people of this area, and announced a "Gala Fireworks Display." Although it was still a little early, at about five o'clock I set out toward one edge of the unnecessarily extensive area a half mile or so northeast of the station where the young man had told me the fireworks would be shot off. A small river about twelve feet wide flowed there, and it had been decided that the embankment of this river would be the most suitable area for setting off the fireworks. Indeed, it was considered *the* place where there would be no danger at all.

The area was covered with summer grass. Some fifteen or twenty tubes, which looked like three-foot clay pipes, had been arranged for the fireworks. The nature of the place and the effect created by the heads of those many tubes jutting up in the grass aroused in me hallucinations of standing in a graveyard. Five or six youths were seated nearby, surrounding the boisterous children. There I encountered a man from the hamlet of our refuge whom I only knew by sight. He told me that a pyrotechnic device which was to be the main attraction tonight was being set up about one hundred yards from where we were standing but still on the embankment; that in order to see this the spectators would be assembling under a steel bridge still another one hundred yards away; and that the people from our hamlet would soon be arriving there.

But possibly because it was still too early, not a single person had yet appeared in the area under the steel bridge which was scheduled as the place for the spectators to assemble. And the sun was still poised over the steel bridge.

"We call this a five-village cooperative project, but only my hamlet shoots the fireworks. That's because we had an old man named Hara who made fireworks, and so our young people learned how to do it," the man said. That was the first I knew of it, but all the young people who were here were from our hamlet.

"You mean Hosen Hara, don't you?" I asked.

"I'm surprised that you know him!" The fellow had a look of amazement as he said this.

"Do you suppose there's anyone who knows him well?"

"Well, I don't know. I guess I knew him, but over there's a man called Tassan who seems to have been Uncle Hosen's disciple in fireworks."

Then he escorted me to the forty-year-old man who

was called Tassan, no one I remembered ever seeing before. When I inquired, he told me that he had been drafted early in the war and had only late last year returned from the Soviet Union. When he spoke, he used language that seemed resentful and unsociable, but he didn't seem a particularly bad man. He spoke awkwardly but liked to speak. Apparently he had a position of over-all responsibility for shooting off today's fireworks, and the young men there snapped to at his every command.

"If you're talking about Uncle Hosen's fireworks, I'd say he got started because he liked them. He was an amateur of course, but he got to be a pro at the rapid-fire. I don't know much about the work done by fireworks makers in town, but . . ." Tassan broke off his sentence in the middle and routed a gang of children who were hanging around. "Well, let's get started," he said to the young men. "Fire two or three more shots to liven things up!"

This was the first time I had ever seen fireworks being shot off. First, one youth dumped into the tube a small amount of gunpowder that had been wrapped in paper. Next, the balls of fireworks were inserted. Then, with a fuse he ignited some solidified gunpowder he held in his hand and tossed it into the tube. Instantly, a white smoke went rushing and swirling up into the heavens, followed by a piercingly loud explosion. I was astonished at this primitive operation.

"I've heard that Uncle Hosen was struggling to produce the color of the bell-flower. Did you know that?" I inquired of Tassan when the noise of the third blast of fireworks had subsided.

"No, I don't know anything about that. To tell you the truth, I have a feeling that I once heard something of that sort, but I don't even have a clear recollection of what I heard either," he replied. "There's one thing I won't forget about that old man though. It was the last time that he ever shot any off . . ."

It was the evening of the last time that Hosen Hara shot any fireworks. Tassan said that on his return home that night he had found that his draft call had come, and for the full six years or more from the time he was drafted until he returned at the end of last year, he had been overseas. Since that was a special occasion, Hosen's fireworks demonstration that night left a marked impression on him, one that he could still remember. In less than one month after that, he was sent to northern China to his first post in Feng-t'ai where his first letters from home had been held for him. Among these letters there was one which came from a friend informing him of Hosen Hara's death.

"When I learned that Uncle Hosen was dead, I had a weird feeling. 'Poor old Hara!' I thought. I had never felt that way about the old man until then, but yet I suddenly realized then that I had known the old man was going to die. And when I thought of the old man shooting off the fireworks, there was something extraordinary about it."

"What do you mean by 'extraordinary'?"

"I guess it's a funny thing to say, but anyhow, even now I can't forget the way the old man looked that night," said Tassan.

The last time he shot off fireworks was at a fireworks festival in 1940, commemorating the 2600th anniversary of the Accession of the Emperor Jimmu, as Tassan remembered it. Something was being inaugurated at that time under the joint sponsorship of several villages, just like today, in the schoolyard to the elementary school of a hamlet two train stops toward Yonago from here. At that time, there was no one else at that place who manufactured fireworks, so Hosen had undertaken the job himself at their request. For two months he had the youths of our hamlet helping him to turn out the fireworks, and he had himself gone to the schoolyard to shoot them off.

"Anyhow, they were amateurish fireworks, so they weren't very interesting. But his rapid-fire was superb," Tassan said, proud of their rapid-fire technique of those days.

On that occasion he had gone ahead and prepared sixty four-inch chrysanthemum balls. Tassan was in charge of passing the balls of fireworks, with Hosen receiving and thrusting them into the tubes at the rate of about twenty shots a minute.

"Generally, in rapid-fire there is hardly any interval between the time the first one going up bursts open and the time you can see the one below going up. Nevertheless, you have to get the next ball into the tube in a steady rhythm without stretching that interval. That's a very tough job."

He said that Hosen was able to do this brilliantly and get away in time, even though he had a hand with three fingers missing. The arena they had used on that occasion was not so extensive as the one we now had. In front of the City Hall right next to the school, traffic was heavy and the roads were filled with thousands of spectators. The whole area was unusually crowded. A place for setting off the fireworks had been erected beside the high-bar in the schoolyard, and Hosen, Tassan, and an additional three or four young men were there. Since these fireworks were the rapid-fire type and they had to thrust the balls into the tubes in rapid succession, the tubes became red-hot and burned out almost instantly and had to be changed. Hosen was so active and agile that you wouldn't have thought he was an old man. When Hosen had finished shooting off the sixty chrysanthemums without any apparent difficulty, he suddenly seemed unable to straighten his back because he had repeated the same action over and over again with his back bent.

With his back still cramped, he had asked Tassan, "How was it? Was it pretty?"

This was because during the time he was shooting off the fireworks himself he had not had time to look up and see them. And when Tassan had answered that they were brilliant, Hosen had lowered himself to the ground, still bent over, panting and short of breath, his head drooped motionlessly, unable to say anything. Apparently this work was too strenuous for a man of his sixty-eight years.

Then a little later, "The spectators . . . they seemed . . . very noisy . . . shouting, weren't they?" he said to Tassan without looking up in his direction.

At these words from Hosen, Tassan at first could hardly recall the din of the crowds, even though he had been there passing the balls to Hosen. Everything that had happened just an instant earlier had seemed to Tassan like the events in a dream. Probably Hosen also had placed himself out of this world—between dream and reality—and after he had finished shooting the fireworks, the noise had vaguely come to life in his mind.

Tassan had told me that he had been left with a strong impression of Hosen that night, and listening to his story I also developed an image of Hosen on that occasion which has somehow persisted in my mind. Taking out a cigarette, I offered one to Tassan. He thanked me and took one, but put it in his shirt pocket.

"We can't smoke here," he said. I had mechanically taken one myself, so I quickly put my cigarette back in the pack.

Then I said that it was seven years since Hosen passed away.

"Yes, that's right. I was thirty-four when I was drafted, and I'm now forty," said Tassan, and then, for no reason at all, he laughed.

"Even the old man . . ." he started to say, but he

suddenly shut his mouth and then, instead, said that it looked like the village association was assembling. I looked toward the steel bridge. Sure enough, headed toward the bridge, several small groups in threes and fives were crossing the elevated ridges of the rice fields or walking along the railroad track and assembling. I looked attentively. The people were approaching slowly, carrying small plain or figured mats or scarves. Only the children were running.

"Even the old man . . ." he had started to say and then had turned silent. That was the way I left Tassan. I walked across the embankment toward the steel bridge so that I could spend as much time as possible with anyone at all I might meet from the hamlet to which we had evacuated. At the western edge of the plain, the sun was now sinking, accentuating the red-soil in the buttes on the sides of the low hills. Already at water level, the red evening sun was shooting arrows of light over the cultivated land in the direction of my destination.

I had the feeling later that even without asking I knew what Tassan had intended to say. Hosen's widow and my wife had a common way of reasoning; both had felt a repugnance toward something about Hosen. So also, Tassan and I both shared in common the opposite view. Even while we did not fully understand the true character of Hosen or find him particularly captivating, we were both attracted to him the way he was on the night he shot off fireworks for the last time.

Thinking these things, I walked off.

VI

THE FOREGOING is what I know of the counterfeiter Hosen Hara. All of it is only fragmentary hearsay that I picked up from people. Somewhere along the line, when all these fragments were pieced together, however, my image of the sixty-eight-year life and career of this counterfeiter emerged as a single cold and dismal stream. And that single stream had a dark and muddled evolution, completely without rhythm and entirely without essence. It was unbearable to think that this person called Hosen Hara was fated by birth to assume that way of life. Unbearable, but also because it was unbearable, it had inherent in it the eerie melancholy of predestination in the fullest sense of *karma*. Whenever I thought about human pathos, I was perforce reminded of a human being—(and at times I thought of Hosen in this light)—a human being who unbeknownst to his wife stealthily wielded the counterfeiter's brush; a human being who furtively, so that his wife wouldn't discover it, twisted gunpowder in paper and ignited it; a human being with a wizened, grayish, shadowy, and lethargic appearance.

However, when I learned of the entry of this person in the unique, hand-written Keigaku diary, I was struck with an entirely different sort of emotion. How strange that the Keigaku who conquered the world and the Hosen who had continued to turn his back to that crowd of spectators without even looking at the fireworks display which he himself had set off—how strange that both of these men had started life from the same position and the same point of departure! Knowing this, I felt for the first time that what I had witnessed in Hosen was not the evolution of a life that was fated to be dismal and muddled, but rather the tragedy of a mediocre man who on contact with a genius had been battered about and crushed by the weight of his best friend. The dismal fatalistic feeling which I had sensed until now in this one counterfeiter's career was extinguished, and the person that was Hosen Hara loomed before me tinged rather with the hue of human tragedy.

If Hosen Hara had not been a friend of Keigaku Onuki, if he had not had an intimate association with him, Hosen's career might have been entirely different, I thought. At some stage Hosen Hara might have gone out into the world of art and might have made his name memorable, perhaps to the point of recognition by the Academy. For some reason I could not help feeling that Keigaku Onuki had played a very decisive role in the hapless career of Hosen Hara; nor do I think that this is just my own arbitrary way of looking at this life. If you consider the Keigaku of the period around 1897, when he wrote that diary, a hidden genius, a dragon lying dormant waiting for the opportunity to soar to ethereal heights, then wasn't Hosen Hara a helpless and hopeless grub-beetle with no other course than to cower before the impact of Keigaku's glorious brilliance? What possible stance could this Hosen in his twenties take in front of the Keigaku who had come to drink with him bearing the silver trophy? And what kind of expression could there have been on the young Hosen's face when, on returning home, he saw the elbaorate characters of the poem Keigaku had written on the door?

The tragedy of this person—discouraged, but with his small eyes still manifesting the vigor of his competitive spirit, his slender jaw and mouth alive with nervousness and jealousy, his skin speckled with the black spots that followed him to his old age, his hairline destined to recede (I had now revised my concept of Hosen's appearance in this way, but anyhow . . .) —the tragedy in that long and dismal career was gradually but in a deep-rooted form already getting underway during the period from 1897 to the summer of 1899.

With this, I conclude my investigation of Hosen Hara for the present. This is because I must proceed with Keigaku's biography to the time when his masterpiece "The Happy Mountain Peak,"* his first work of that period, appeared and to an account of the vigorous activities of his middle period which fixed his position in the art world.

During those two days that I gazed fixedly at the summit of Mount Amagi without touching my pen to Keigaku's biography, the red buds of the crape myrtle at the edge of the garden had suddenly diminished and its white blossoms were in bloom. Perhaps I only imagined it, but the rising cumulus summer clouds constantly rolling upward had changed to wispy autumn clouds drifting unnoticeably away. I looked at the calendar; it was the First Day of Autumn.

Even then I remembered the Hosen Hara forgeries of Keigaku's "Flowers and Birds" and "The Fox" which had hung in the *tokonoma* of the two farmhouses in the mountain-ridge hamlet in the Chugoku range where the atmosphere of autumn had similarly begun to fill the air. And at that moment those same thoughts of the Eternal seized me once again. Eternity was something related to Keigaku and Hosen, and yet, ironically, Life held one small reality which was irrelevant to both Keigaku and Hosen: in that mountain hamlet originals and forgeries had no meaning. When fall came I would go to Kyoto and drink saké with Takuhiko Onuki and tell him about the aspects of Hosen which he didn't know, I thought. And at that moment, I became submerged in my thoughts which sparkled with a cold light.

* A euphemism for Mount Fuji.

OBASUTE

OBASUTE

I

WHEN ON earth was it that I first heard the legends about abandoning the old people on Mount Obasute?

I come from a mountain village in the central part of the Izu Peninsula. There I was educated during my childhood days. In the Toi region on the west coast of the peninsula, tales about discarding old folks in the mountains in ancient times have been handed down from generation to generation. In all likelihood, it was along with these tales that I heard the Legend of Mount Obasute, a mountain whose very name means to discard old people, and it caused my small heart to swell with sorrow.

Wasn't I about five or six at that time? On hearing that story I went out onto a porch and screamed and sobbed. I have no recollection of where that place was exactly, but what I do recall in my faint memory is that my grandmother—or was it my mother?—anyhow, a member of my family immediately came flying out to the porch and said something to me—just a few words. Of course, I could not comprehend the story itself, but the sadness of the whole idea of carrying my mother on my back and taking her up a mountain and abandoning her there became an abstraction which oozed into my heart like waterdrops dripping between rocks. I shrieked and cried, unable to endure the sorrow of being separated from my mother.

It was only after I became ten or eleven that I was able

to grasp the full meaning of the story of Mount Obasute in its entirety. Occasionally I used to get picture books from an aunt of mine who lived in a small town about twenty miles away. In one of those volumes there was a tale called *Obasute-Yama*. Apparently all sorts of variations of the legend about abandoning old folks on Mount Obasute are in circulation with slightly altered details. But the one that I know is based entirely on that book, and it continues to hold to this day without modification. It can easily be discerned how strong an impression that picture book *Obasute-Yama* imprinted on my mind when I was a child. Of all the tales that I heard in my childhood, the two that I can't forget even now are the story of Ishidomaru, who went to visit his father on Mount Koya, and the Legend of Mount Obasute. Both have as their themes the anguish of separation of a parent and child.

Years later, during my university days, when I was back home on summer vacation, I fortuitously rediscovered this *Obasute-Yama* picture book in the cupboard of our godown, and I looked it over again. Only the frontispiece was in color; the illustrations on several other pages were in black-and-white relief; and the Legend of Obasute was written in a literary style that might be considered a little too difficult for children.

In ancient times in the Province of Shinano there was a feudal lord who hated old people. So he decreed throughout the land that when old people became seventy years of age, they were, without exception, to be taken to the mountains and left there. One bright moon-lit night a young farmer climbed up a mountain carrying his mother on his back. Since his mother had reached the age of seventy, he had to discard her there. However, the young man could not bear the thought of leaving her there—no matter what! He brought her back home again, dug a hole under the floor so no one would see her, and hid her there. About this time, an envoy from a neighboring province appeared before the feudal lord and laid down a very difficult proposal. He posed three problems, and if these were not solved, the Province of Shinano would be attacked and destroyed. The three problems were: to make a rope out of ashes; to pass a thread through a nine-sided jewel; and to make a drum beat by itself. The feudal lord was perplexed, and he issued a proclamation throughout the land calling upon the wise men to solve these difficult problems. When the young farmer told this to his mother, who was hidden under the floor, the mother instantly explained to him how the problems could be solved. The young farmer immediately went to the home of the feudal lord and told him. Because of this the province was able to be saved from its difficulties. On learning from the young man that all this was due to the wisdom of an old woman, the feudal lord became enlightened and understood that old people should be respected, and without any further hesitation he proceeded to abolish the decree.

So went the story.

The colored frontispiece was a drawing of a young man wearing a hood like the headgear of court nobles. Carrying his aged mother on his back, he was making his way through the thick underbrush as he climed up a steep mountain. The mother's hair was white but her face seemed exceedingly young, so that the combination produced a slightly weird effect. The rays of the full moon tinted the entire scene blue everywhere—the trees and grass and earth—and the shadows of the two people were imprinted in bold relief in black over the ground like spilled ink. It was just a coarse, common picture, but even so the sadness inherent in the story and the scene still rose from the superficies of the character of the picture. For the minds of children, it was probably adequately stimulating.

The months and years flew by. I left the university. About the time I first started working at a newspaper company, I got hold of a volume entitled *New Thoughts about Mount Obasute* and read it. At that time, I must say, I lacked the patience to read books with any substance; but in a desultory sort of way I usually just dabbled capriciously in any of the miscellaneous books that happened to come my way. It was entirely by a stroke of good luck at the time that I chanced upon this monograph *New Thoughts about Mount Obasute*, which was one of the "Publications of the Shinano Topographical Society," and I set it aside in my library.

The evening that I bought it, I looked thoroughly over the first part of the volume, lost interest in the later sections, and closed the book. Even at that, however, I was able to acquire a certain amount of knowledge of the thinking with regard to Mount Obasute, knowledge which could not possibly be of any earthly use to me as a reporter.

As a result of the labors of the author of *New Thoughts about Mount Obasute*, I learned:

that the Mount Obasute legends about abandoning elderly people first appeared as literature in the *Tales of Yamato*;

that these tales concerning the disposal of old people probably were imported from India but set in a local environment and were transplanted into Japan along with the importation of Buddhism;

that apart from these importations, the practice of *obasute* must have existed in Japan in very ancient times;

that legends about the practice of *obasute* had been handed down in the oral tradition of every province, but except for the Legend of Mount Obasute of Shinano Province, into which many of the other legends were incorporated, the others have all been lost;

that, presumably, the fact that Mount Obasute became

famous as a moon-viewing site in itself contributed to the assimilation of all such legends into the Legend of Mount Obasute;

that, furthermore, the *obasute* practice itself had been attributed to different mountains in various historical eras—Obase-yama,* in ancient times; Kamuriki-yama, in the Middle Ages;

that it was only in modern times that the area around Obasute Station on the Shinonoi Railway Line emerged for the first time under the name of Mount Obasute.

These things I learned from the travails of the author of *New Thoughts about Mount Obasute.*

After the passage of several more years, I read the book again for an entirely different purpose, (incidentally, assembled in this book there were virtually all the *haiku* and *tanka* relating to moon-viewing at Mount Obasute by all the great poets in the literary history of Japan) because I was interested in determining how the various famous poets dealt with the same subject, moon-viewing against the backdrop of the same setting, Sarashina. From this point of view, I guess I had a pretty punctilious concern about such matters.

The *haiku,* excerpts from several collections such as *Obasute and Lotus* and *Cutting Rice-Plants,* were assembled from the works of a host of *haiku*-poets led by Basho, Buson, Issa, and others. The *tanka* were selected only from poems which thematicized Mount Obasute, but they were drawn from anthologies of every era and included the names of such poets as Tsurayuki, Saigyo, Sanetomo, Teika, and Norinaga.

But what I remember as being the most deeply moving among all these great *haiku* and *tanka* was one which the young man who appears in the *Tales of Yamato* composed

* The near resemblance in sound of these two names is coincidental; *obase,* which means something like "little valley" has no connection with the meaning of *obasute.*

as he watched the moon hanging over Mount Obasute after returning home from leaving his mother on the mountain. The poem goes:

> *Seeing the clear moon*
> *Hang o'er Mount Obasute,*
> *Oh, Sarashina!*
> *What solace is there for me—*
> *How can my heart be consoled?*

Leaving aside the entire question of the skill of execution of the poem itself, I could visualize this one as a poem by the hero of the story and not simply a moon-viewing verse, and the drama behind it gripped me.

From the pure aesthetics of *tanka* of course, its value probably could be questioned, but more than any work on moon-viewing at Mount Obasute, this poem by the man in the story stirred me immensely. The theme of this tale, which had been etched on my heart during my childhood, returned to me transformed here as a poem.

II

FOR A LONG time I really knew nothing about either Obasute Station on the Shinonoi Line or the immediately surrounding area. I had made trips in that direction, but mostly I came to that area at night, or even if it was during the day, I passed the station without noticing it and never had any particular connection with it.

It was my mother who sometime later provided me with the occasion to recall the Legend of Mount Obasute. Apropos of nothing, my mother suddenly said, "They say that Mount Obasute's a famous place for moon-viewing, so the old folks may have been quite happy even though they were abandoned there. If even now there was an ordinance that old people had to be gotten rid of, I'd go happily. I think it would be just fine to be able to live alone. Besides, if you have to be discarded, you may even get used to it."

My mother was just seventy. Her words grated on the ears of the members of my family who heard them just like sarcasm. My younger brother and sisters were also there at the time, and they all took on expressions of surprise and shock. This occurred at a time when there were those post-war shortages of everything; it was a time when the general attitude toward the family system showed signs of hysterical change, and there were all those petty disputes that happen between the young people and the old men and women. My family was certainly no exception, but by this I do not mean that every problem was of such magnitude as to make my mother consider escaping from the family, so to speak. My mother, realizing that she had just reached seventy, the age to be left in the mountains in the world of *obasute* legends, presumably because of the strength of her pride and the spirit of stalwartness with which she was born, took it into her head instantly to defy the atmosphere of this post-war period which so closely resembled something in those legends.

Like the old character depicted in that children's picture book, my mother's hair was white, but she had a bright youthful complexion and there wasn't a single wrinkle in her face. For a while, I eyed her face without a word. She had been raised with a dislike for old people, but now she herself was chronologically a creditably old woman. I felt a compassion for this mother of mine who had become so conscious of her old age and had such a defiant attitude about it. Curiously, from then on, I became obsessed by the whole setting of the Shinano *obasute* story.

Shortly after that I had many opportunities to take trips in connection with my work, and several times a year I had to go to the Shinano area. When I used the Chuo Line, I often passed the small Obasute Station nestled in among the hills. It became impossible for me to regard with the same dispassion as I viewed the scenery at other places either the Zenkoji Plain, which opens out from there in a vast expanse, or the Chikuma River, which meanders over that plain in a thousand curves, as its name implies, glittering with a cold luster like the belly of a snake. On the other hand, sometimes I took the Shin-etsu Line. Since trains on this line run along the low-lying plain which I used to look out across from the Chuo Line, on reaching the area around Togura, above the window sill I could spot the slope of the hill opposite Obasute Station, which I could just about identify by the red roof of the station. Always, as I looked out across that whole stretch of land in this vicinity, I was filled with a sort of emotion as I wondered about things connected with *obasute*.

I of course had practically no interest in Obasute as a moon-viewing site. True enough, I recognized that there undoubtedly was a splendor in looking at the moon filling the clear Shinano air and shining across the entire panorama of the open country which contained the Chikuma and Sai Rivers, but I didn't believe that the Obasute moon could ever surpass the moon I had watched shining over the bleak flatlands of Manchuria during the war. Without exception, when I passed through the vicinity around Obasute, a deep emotion began to take hold of me—that my aged mother was certainly sitting up there. One time, when I passed Obasute Station, there floated before my eyes an apparition of me tramping around in that area carrying my mother on my back.

Of course, the setting is in ancient times. I do not see the flourish of modern homes which dot the hillocks at the foot of the mountain and extend out over the bleak plain. Besides, it is night and the moonbeams are falling, blue over the surrounding area, just like in the illustration in the *Obasute-Yama* picture book. Only my mother's shadow and mine are black.

"Where on earth do you say you'll leave me?" asks my mother.

She is past seventy and her entire body has become miniscule. Her body is so light that it is depressing, but nevertheless I am tired anyhow, exhausted from walking around all over with a human being on my back. There is a giddiness in my legs with every step I take.

"How about here?" I ask. "If I build a small hut around here . . ."

"A place like *this?* Ugh!" My mother has a young voice. Her body is frail but she is strong-willed, and not the slightest abatement in her uncompromising nature shows through even under circumstances like these, when I'm in the process of abandoning her. "Isn't it dangerous beside the cliffs when it rains? What if there are landslides? I wonder if there isn't a more sensible place?"

"I don't think so. Your demands are too extravagant, Mama. Still, how would it be if I rented the outhouse of that temple we just saw?"

"Oh, no! No! No!" Mother, on my back, kicks her feet and pounds with her hands like a spoiled child. "There would be lots of mosquitoes there in the summer. Besides, the building is old. And wouldn't that room be dark and gloomy? You're unkind. Really you are!"

I am bewildered, at a loss.

"If that's the case," say I, "I'd just as soon take you back home again. I don't know why it wouldn't be better to go back home to a crowded, noisy place with everybody around rather than to be here in a place like this."

"Again you're talking like that! Now that I've purposely left home, I wouldn't return for anything in the world.

I wouldn't be back with everybody again for anything. I don't like the people at home; I don't like the people in the village. I only have a few years left, so I won't be satisfied unless I'm allowed to live alone and do as I please."

"You're just like a spoiled child. You really are, Mama."

"Then I'm a spoiled child. It's my nature to be spoiled, so I can't help it. Even so, you just look me in the face and say 'you're spoiled, you're spoiled!' What's 'spoiled' about being abandoned?"

"Damn!"

" 'Damn' all you want, but I'm not going back home. So hurry up and get rid of me."

"Even if I *wanted* to get rid of you, the problem is that I can't find a suitable place for you."

"You can't find one if you don't look for it. You won't be punished for looking for a place to leave your mother!"

"Didn't I just walk my feet off looking all this time? You probably realize that I'm staggering. I wonder just how far I *have* walked. We've gone to see ten houses already."

"But I don't fancy any of them. Was there a single house that looked habitable to *you?*"

"So, I've given up trying to rent a house. I said I would find a place that suited you and would build a hut for you, didn't I? But you complain wherever I go."

" 'Complain,' you say! I'm an old woman. Oh, I wonder if there really is any place where I can live quietly alone. Couldn't you look harder? Oh! My back hurts! Couldn't you carry me on your back somehow so I'd be more comfortable? It's gotten cold! It feels as if the moonbeams are making my skin prickle."

"Be still, please, Mama, and don't kick up such a fuss. I'm tired too. It's fine for you, Mama. You're getting carried, but I'm the one who's doing the carrying, huh?

Please, I beg you. Please, let's just go back home. It'll be a relief to everybody."

"No," snaps my mother.

"I don't understand your no's. We're not going to wander around like this all night. Honestly, we're going back home." When I say that, my mother raises her weak voice in a sudden and drastic change.

"Show a little bit of patience. Just in this, show a little bit of patience. All you want to do is take me home. I won't say anything else. Anything at all will be fine with me. Just leave me. You won't have to call me 'spoiled.' Over there you can see a hut. That one will be fine too. Just leave me there."

"Just a little while ago when we looked at that hut, didn't you say it was drafty and cold and that, besides, it leaks when it rains?"

"It doesn't particularly appeal to me, but that can't be helped. I'll put up with it. It's a house and secluded, and I possibly can live in it quietly and free from all worries and cares."

"But it's awful there. As your child, I can't leave you there."

"It doesn't matter to me if it's awful. Now hurry, go ahead and leave me there," says my mother. Then, as I linger there, the moonbeams bite their way into my body.

This is the sort of play-act I imagined taking place with my mother. My conversations with my mother coursed smoothly and naturally through my brain. My mother is spoiled, but there is a look of real earnestness on her face. Reality breaks through to me as I am being badgered by my mother—"Go ahead and leave me; go ahead and leave me; go ahead . . ."

It was strange how really naturally a character resembling my mother had been fused into the mother of my vision. This visionary one-act play—with me serving as the stage for this *obasute*-drama—was fairly far removed from the theme of the Legend of Obasute on which it was patterned because, in my case, it was the wish of the mother herself to be abandoned; because she persisted in saying that she wanted to be left and then did not agree to anything; and because I remained there carrying my mother on my back as I wandered around the Obasute hills. But that strangeness in particular, I felt, had set something like a small lump of ice somewhere in my heart. But when that funny feeling had vanished, in its stead chills spread all over my body.

It was awful to have imagined my mother badgering me about wanting to be left. But, perhaps, imagining such a scene as this in which I was abandoning my mother might have been a way of getting something off my chest.

Even so, why did I imagine my mother like that? I have often thought about this for long periods of time. And I have tried putting myself on my own back in place of my mother. And I have thought that when I get to be an old man, I may be just like the mother of my vision.

III

THIS SUMMER, I went to deliver a lecture at a coal-mining town on the bank of the Enga River in northern Kyushu. There, at a Japanese-style inn, I met my younger sister Kiyoko whom I hadn't seen for two years. Kiyoko is the youngest of the four children in our family. She was married during the war and had two children, but there had been some sort of incident and she had fled from her husband's house, leaving him and the two children; for a while she returned to our parents' home;

but now she had fled from that too on the grounds that she wanted to make her own way of life.

Even since I was small, I had liked this sister best of all my brothers and sisters, but I felt that there was something unpardonable in her selfish behavior. It wasn't anything like a cardinal sin, anything worth breaking relations over or never speaking to each other again—but Kiyoko, with her innate sensitivity, apparently realizing how I felt, did not write me a single letter after leaving home. For my part, all I even knew about her now was that she was working in northern Kyushu.

When I decided to make the trip to Kyushu, however, I considered going to see my sister. Accordingly, before I left Tokyo, I asked my mother for her address and sent her a telegram saying that I wanted to meet her. "Kiyoko might come to meet me, and then again she might not come," I thought.

That night when I returned to the inn from the lecture hall, my sister was sitting in a corner of my room near the veranda. Her face was brighter than I expected; her figure was trim; she was wearing a grey skirt and a pure-white sweater; her hair was cut fashionably short. While she actually was thirty-four years old, at first glance she looked as if she was only twenty-four or twenty-five.

"As far as my living goes, well, I'm eating—but I'm not living in luxury," said Kiyoko.

Her present job was at a beauty parlor at the air base in a coastal town near the mouth of the Enga River. There, Kiyoko had somehow or other come to be in charge of several girls who were around twenty years old, and she was working catering to foreign women.

We talked along lines that I guess were appropriate enough for a brother and sister who had not seen each other for a long time. There were many things that I, from the standpoint of being her older brother, could have said—about her separation from her family and about her behavior since then—but I didn't touch on these subjects at all. All of those things were problems about which nothing much could be done any more. Because she had run away from home even at the cost of leaving her two children, I felt that she must be a very resolutely strong-minded woman, a woman unto herself, with her own reasons for what she did.

I only chose matters concerning our parents and our brother and sister to talk about.

"Mama's still acting that way about *obasute*," I said.

Ever since the time when our mother had said that she wanted to be left at Obasute, the term *obasute* had been used by my brothers and sisters and me when we were talking amongst ourselves. It was a convenient word for us to use. Actually, it was just like my mother to say that she wanted to be left at Obasute—she was likely to say this at any time—and this illustrated both the best that was in her and the worst. Nevertheless, inherent in the words "still acting that way about *obasute*," there was some implied mild criticism of Mama's pride and her spoiled and unreasonable nature. On the other hand, for her children, who were able to accept the fact that she was all of these things, the phrase also embraced a feeling of sympathy toward her.

At my words, there was a look on Kiyoko's face for a moment as if she were biting her lips to restrain some oncoming laughter, but she only said, "Talking about *obasute*, I wonder if at that time Mama didn't mean that she really wanted to be left on Mount Obasute."

"Why?"

"Why? Just because I felt that way. I honestly wonder if she didn't really want to be left by herself, to get entirely away from constantly becoming involved in everything that was happening around her, to be left alone in the mountains somewhere."

"Aw, cut it out!" said I, rather thoughtlessly. There

was something in the way Kiyoko spoke that somehow startled me.

"Was that your impression even way back then?"

"No. It just came to me now. When you used the word *"obasute"* I suddenly got that impression—just now."

I again began to visualize the scene in that vision of mine when I was wandering about in the vicinity of Obasute carrying my mother on my back. And at the thought of it, I felt shivers come over me for a second time, just as they had then.

As if she had been thinking this matter over for a while, Kiyoko a bit later said, "In my case, I had that kind of feeling too when I ran away from home. It was like this—how should I put it?—I just had to be alone, to get away immediately and completely from all the annoyances, so . . ."

"So, you too wanted to be left alone—*obasute*-style?"

"Well . . ."

"But you make such a *young* grandma."

"Yes, it'll still be quite a while before I'm seventy."

Then and only then did Kiyoko smile, but it was a sad smile. I could have taken all this to mean that she was obliquely using this conversation of ours to justify her own past behavior, but on the other hand, her real attitude at the time might very well have been something completely different from that.

About the children whom she had deserted I said nothing. She too may have wanted to make some passing reference to the children, but she acted as though she was well able to endure not talking about them.

If Kiyoko had said she was worried about the children, I would have had no alternative but to tell her that this was natural but that she should have known from the start that such would be the case. She knew that—and I did too.

She stayed overnight with me, sharing my room. Like

so many inns at these coal-mining villages, the building had all sorts of labyrinthine annexes lumped together under one roof, and there must have been a banquet or something going on in a section somewhere off in the distance. The sounds of a *samisen*, the loud voices of men, and charming feminine voices could be heard until very late.

The next morning I went down to the station with my sister to see her off. It would take her about an hour to get back to her place by electric train. Although it was early in the morning, the sooty streets were already filled with lots of people walking around. It was a town of about sixty thousand, but according to what the maid at the inn said, it was in a constant state of flux, and if you added the suburbs, the population would probably be about double that figure. To be sure, the same restlessness that seemed to fill the streets was also to be found in the make-up of the stores on both sides of the avenue and in the way the pedestrians moved about. The smoke that came pouring out of the chimneys of the briquet factories was clouding up the sky and making the air murky.

En route, as I walked along the road beside my sister, I could see two huge pyramidal slag heaps. Kiyoko told me that slag heaps like these could also be seen along the railway line of the electric train she was about to take.

After we arrived at the station and just before she went through the gate, Kiyoko said with a sort of slight melancholy smile, "You know, I'd like to go back to Tokyo. But, for the time being . . ."

"If you had the same kind of work, wouldn't you be just as well off in Tokyo?"

There was a quizzical expression on her face. "But if I work here a while longer, I'll acquire some real skill at this. When I say that it's because I'm getting good as this work—I mean—I think it's better here because I'm working with foreigners."

It occurred to me that apart from the question of acquiring technical proficiency, Kiyoko probably felt that she wanted to live somewhat isolated from the home she had deserted.

"I wondered if I was going to be scolded severely and I was nervous about coming—but I'm glad I came," she said.

"I wouldn't scold you. Scolding doesn't undo what's been done, does it?"

"Is it all right if I write to you from now on?" she asked.

"There's no question of its being all right or not all right."

"Well then . . ."

Kiyoko slipped through the gate as though she were escaping. She raised her right hand and waved it, just from the wrist. She was like a little girl. Her conduct was not that of a woman who had suffered.

As there were still about two hours before I was to depart from this town with the group that came down with me, I passed through the main street and strolled over to the edge of town. The place was jam-packed with restaurants, inns, and *pachinko* parlors, and that was all there was to see. Since I had heard the previous day from the people of this area that sometimes the ground around here caved in and houses toppled because there had been mines under this town, I walked with caution, but I didn't encounter any such toppling houses. But here and there, while I was at the edge of town, I did come across puddles of all dimensions. And I wondered if these too weren't because of the depressions which resulted when the ground caved in. This Chikuho coal-belt continues right on northward to the sea coast, and my sister has just gone back to the beauty parlor at the air base on that sea coast, I thought.

My sister had taken a very womanish point of view toward my mother's attitude of wanting to be abandoned on Mount Obasute. But when I thought about this, there seemed a bit more justification for Kiyoko to be spending almost two years in a corner of the Kyushu coalfield belt watching the moon come out over an *obasute-yama* designed out of coal and possessing man-made artificiality.

Suddenly, I stopped in my tracks. Ever since Kiyoko had said something yesterday, I had felt as though there was something I had to ponder. It was an uneasy feeling, but right now I felt that the true nature of what I had to ponder was suddenly flashing in my brain in a clear form. Mightn't it be said that the idea that had once come over my mother—that she wanted to be left at Obasute—was obviously a form of pessimism toward life? And for whatever reasons she might have had, didn't Kiyoko's pessimistic disposition, which was somewhat of the same nature as Mama's, play a role in her desertion of her family, which is something that just doesn't happen to ordinary people?

As I thought about this, I also recalled an incident involving my younger brother, Shoji. It happened during the third year after the end of the war. One day Shoji, who at that time was working in the political department of one of the leading newspapers, came to have dinner with me at my place. At the bus stop when he was going home, he said to me, "I've suddenly become fed up with the newspaper office. This kind of work didn't suit my nature right from the beginning, but recently it's gotten so terrible that I can't stand it. I think I'd like to switch completely to a job where there's much less contact with people."

90

Shoji, from every angle, had a bright disposition, good for attracting friends. At first glance he seemed just perfect as a newspaper reporter, so such talk, which seemed suddenly to reveal what was deep down in his heart, surprised me. I recognized, however, that newspaper work had now really gotten on his nerves. And I realized that my brother must doubtless have had this sort of attitude ever since childhood.

"If you dislike it that much, wouldn't it be a good idea to quit and change to some other line of work?"

"I want to. Honestly."

"Go ahead. You're still young."

I spoke as though I were almost advising him to do that. It was not out of irresponsibility that I did so; it was just that there was something about my brother at that time that made it impossible for me to say anything else.

About two months later Shoji formally resigned from the newspaper company, moved to a city in the vicinity of his wife's parental home, and got a job at a small bank there. It occurred to me that his personality, which might even be characterised as misanthropic and which he had so unexpectedly revealed to me, would not change at the small local bank any more than it had at the newspaper company. But Shoji is working there to this day.

Even in Shoji's case—he too had developed in such a way that he suddenly wanted to withdraw quietly from a society in which masses of people were crowded up against each other. Wasn't that the driving force in his mind, just as with my mother and sister? Had it turned out that misanthropic blood like that flowed through the veins of all the members of my family? I have still another relative on my mother's side who attempted to shut himself off from his environment.

My mother's brother, the one next down the line in age, or to put it another way, my uncle who has just passed the age of sixty, is also a person who behaved similarly, changing his job suddenly and voluntarily. In spite of the fact that he had acquired some status as a successful man in the position of president of a civil engineering company, for no apparent reason at all, he retired immediately after the end of the war. Completely without rhyme or reason, he carried out this resignation as if to say that he couldn't stand it any longer and was running off. Sometimes my uncle advanced a plausible explanation to the effect that as the president of a small company he couldn't really earn a living and that confrontations with subordinate personnel had become extremely unpleasant for him. Viewed by outsiders, his position was completely incomprehensible, but if this was to be explained in more understandable terms, one needed only to recall his sudden feelings of antipathy toward the environment which he felt was closing in around him. My uncle thereafter started two or three businesses with a little capital, a patent-medicine business, a general store, and maybe something else, but it certainly cannot be said that things went well with any of these. Like my mother, he was a person of strong pride who never complained about how badly things were going, but it was pathetic to watch him.

I could not say that I myself do not have that kind of blood coursing through my body. In a meaningless sort of way, I felt a certain compassion for both Kiyoko and Shoji, and I could apparently also arrive at some understanding of my uncle, even with respect to his suffering and changing from job to job. For doing what they did rather than behaving unlike themselves, I loved them.

I came to the end of the street and walked around a block alongside the miners' homes and continued to think about such things.

IV

It was this fall that I actually set foot on the soil of Obasute myself. I had gone to Shiga Heights in connection with my work, and on the way back I suddenly took it into my head to take a stab at visiting the place called Obasute. It was evening when I got off the train at Togura Station on the Shin-etsu Line. There I stayed overnight at a hot-springs Japanese inn, and the next day I hired a car and headed for Obasute Station.

After leaving the town of Togura, the car followed the bank of the Chikuma River heading downstream, but on leaving this route we started to climb a small hillock.

"It better not rain, huh?" said the middle-aged driver. The sky was dark and overcast, and the weather was chilly. It looked as if it were going to rain.

The mountains along the route that the car took were all bedecked in autumn colors. Before and behind the car the various types of yellow-brown serrate-leafed oaks exuded a redness as if they were aflame, and intermittently there was just the green of pine trees.

We passed two or three hamlets. They were tiny hamlets, all affiliated with the township of Sarashina. Beside each of the houses in these hamlets there was a field where large white radishes and onions had been planted.

As we were passing a hamlet called Uo, we saw five or six old women walking in the road up ahead. The women moved off the road and stood there at the side, waiting for the car to pass.

"Lots of old women, aren't there? Must have been abandoned," I said jokingly.

"Not very likely," said the driver. "If they got left in this area, they could all go back home!"

"In the old days, it was probably very deserted in this area," I ventured.

"I'm sure this was a pretty deserted road. But, it does no good to abandon anybody here with villages so nearby. They still call the area around here Obasute, but the real Mount Obasute is Mount Kamuriki. You can't see it from here, but pretty soon we'll come to a place where you can."

The Mount Kamuriki the driver was talking about was the *obasute-yama* of the Middle Ages, as I knew from the *tanka*. "What about Mount Obase?" I asked, but the driver appeared not to know anything at all about the *obasute-yama* of Early Ancient Times. Or perhaps Mount Obase was currently called something else.

In about thirty minutes the car reached Obasute Station. At the square in front of the station, I got out of the car, and ushered on by the driver, I headed down the road alongside the station toward Choraku Temple, which is known to be a famous moon-viewing site. Step by step we walked right into the scene that I had viewed so often from train windows.

Everywhere the mountains and fields before my eyes were an autumnal red. As we were descending the fairly rapid slope ahead of us, the driver looked back over his shoulder as though he had just remembered something which he had forgotten until then.

"That's Mount Kamuriki" he informed me. There, looking as though it had been piled up beyond the hill, halfway up whose slope that station stood, was a part of the form of Mount Kamuriki, its summit enveloped in clouds. I did not know whether or not this was the *obasute-yama* of the Legend of Obasute, but in any case this Mount Kamuriki was much too high and distant a mountain for people to be able to climb easily. Mama too, if she saw this mountain, probably would not say even jokingly that she wanted to be left on that mountain, I thought.

However, I immediately changed my mind. In my mind, thought I, I had arbitrarily envisioned my own *obasute-yama* and had pictured myself wandering around there carrying Mama on my back. But Mama—being Mama and being completely different from me—might very well have imagined her *obasute-yama* as a big steep mountain like Mount Kamuriki.

In the first place, an *obasute-yama* ought to be a mountain like this one. Come to think of it, even the *obasute-yama* into which Kiyoko had flung herself, and Shoji's too, must certainly have been much closer to the percipitous Mount Kamuriki than they were to the gently rolling hillocks adorned with autumnal colors over which I had just now been strolling.

As we went down the slanting road, I noticed that the slope of the hillock was swarming with stone monuments on which poems had been engraved. Since the letters on the faces of these stones were eroded, I couldn't tell how old or new they were. But the *tanka* and *haiku* and Chinese-style poems which were inscribed on the stones must have been written in appreciation of the bright moon as seen from here. I proceeded down the road and again found that a number of poem-inscribed stones had been erected here and there all over the slope. When I envisioned these stones illuminated by moonbeams, for some reason they gave an uncanny feeling completely irrelevant to their elegance and taste.

Fairly soon the road ended in a gigantic boulder which, by its nature, in itself constituted a precipice. This rock is called Ubaishi—The Old Woman Rock. They say that this is an old woman turned to stone. This rock too was uncanny. But the prospect of Zenjoji Plain, which I could see by standing on this rock, was beautiful with the Chikuma River flowing through the center of the flatlands, the hamlets here and there dotting the solid yellow plain, and the mountains on the opposite side of the Chikuma aflame with the colors of fall.

The steep stone steps alongside the Ubaishi were covered with little maple leaves red as blood, and the narrow precincts of Choraku Temple at the foot of the steps were covered with the yellow leaves of gingko trees. Even when we called out, there wasn't a single sound of anyone emerging from the interior of the priests' living quarters, though there were several children playing in front of them.

We entered a small building, a moon-viewing hall, and rested there. The faces of the votive tablets and votive pictures were all worn away because of the long passage of years. These things were now nothing more than musty old white plates.

"The fall colors seem better than the moon, don't you think?" said my driver. Right then, I had had exactly the same thought.

A corner of the plain was quickly becoming obscured, and just as I was thinking that I heard the sounds of an approaching shower, raindrops began to fall right where we were. We left the place.

That night, I stayed over at the Togura inn. And I wrote a letter to Kiyoko suggesting that she at least seriously consider working in Tokyo. At midnight the shower turned into a downpour.

THE FULL MOON

THE FULL MOON
(Mangetsu)

I

NOTHING in the career or Miyuki Kagebayashi was as significant and as memorable as the harvest-moon night of 1950. Whenever a Stockholders' General Meeting took place in the company's V.I.P. room, it was always the practice to have the company officers join in the social reception which was held afterwards at one of the best southside Japanese restaurants. Even in the case of that day's Emergency General Meeting, there was to be no exception to this policy. There were as many as thirty-eight persons arranged in a U-shape in the banquet hall of the new building of the southside restaurant, where these receptions had been held once or twice before.

Company President Yunoshin Otaka was up front with his back to the *tokonoma*. Seated flanking him were the two big stockholders, the President of the S——Securities Company and the Managing Director of the A——Bank. Kagebayashi sat next to the Managing Director of the Bank. The remaining places up front were occupied by the Directors, and the whole array of Division Chiefs and Section Chiefs was arranged along both arms of the U. Kagebayashi, whose place until now had always been at one end of the Directors' seats, had been moved up closer to the center. With that one exception, the order was the same as before.

The place had a slightly different atmosphere than usual. There were almost the same number of geisha scattered among the guests; but although the banquet had already been underway for almost an hour, there was just a little burst of commotion in one corner, and elsewhere nothing much was going on. Occasionally a shrill cackling and chattering arose from one or another section where the junior officers were, but it seemed entirely out of harmony with the rest of the atmosphere, as though a little firecracker had inadvertently gone off, and afterwards only the cold sound of dishes banging together echoed through the room.

No one knew why the group of Division Chiefs and Section Chiefs, who were lined up on both sides of the U, weren't as boisterous as they usually were. While they were eating and drinking, they would occasionally joke with each other, but mostly they just shot glances sideways down the table toward the abstaining big-shots up front. A strangely uneasy mood pervaded the place.

For some unknown reason the geisha knew right from the beginning that something not so funny was going on at that banquet. From the time they had first entered the banquet hall, shuffling along in two rows like a procession of Peking ducks, and had gone to take their places opposite their guests, the women quickly and perceptively sized up the situation and recognized that there was a tenseness in the atmosphere of that room.

When the sliding doors opened, revealing the dancing stage which seemed unpleasantly and overly white under the fluorescent lights, President Otaka suddenly left his place. The old man, who wore a double-breasted suit in the finest taste and who was famous for always being well-dressed and irascible, bowed ever-so-slightly and, passing behind the group up front, went out of the banquet room into the hallway. He had a competely expressionless look on his face as he walked off toward the entrance.

When he saw the President leaving, Kagebayashi

assumed that Otaka was undoubtedly going home. For Otaka this had certainly not been a very pleasant banquet, and he must have realized more than anyone else that this banquet could not liven up so long as he stayed there. Kagebayashi paid his compliments to the short Bank Manager beside him, who had great signatory powers in the company, and said, "I probably ought to go along with Otaka-san tonight. I think I'll go with him."

The Bank Manager in his naturally husky voice told him that would be fine and to go ahead. Kagebayashi made a slight bow of respect toward the President of the Securities Company and then left unobtrusively so that the others would pay no attention to him. There had been a good reason for his saying "Otaka-san" instead of calling Otaka "*shacho.*" There was no longer any reason for using the term *shacho,* or president. To come right out with it—just three hours earlier Otaka had ceased to be the *shacho,* and Kagebayashi himself had taken his place as the company president. Thus Kagebayashi confirmed that he was by nature the kind of person who would call his superior "Otaka-san" the moment he had ceased to be the *shacho.*

Kagebayashi followed Otaka to the entrance. When he got there, Otaka was sitting on a step at the threshold having his shoestrings tied by Teruko, the younger sister of the woman who owned this restaurant. Two or three of the Division and Section Chiefs had happened to discover that Otaka was leaving, appeared at the door of the dining room, and came out to the threshold.

Kagebayashi also put his shoes on and went out of the vestibule as though he too were leaving, but he did not get into the car with Otaka. Instead, he ordered Teruko to dispatch Otaka's car and to send for his own.

"Oh? Are you leaving?" the astonished Teruko asked.

It was all so strange to see Kagebayashi, who under most circumstances had been like Otaka's shadow and never left his side, usher Otaka more or less brusquely into a car and send him home in the car alone. Even beyond that, it surpassed all comprehension to have Kagebayashi himself leave a banquet early, and alone.

Kagebayashi waited in front of the entrance for two or three minutes until his car came. On leaving the banquet hall he had stated that he was going to accompany Otaka, so he felt somewhat embarrassed about staying behind after sending the erstwhile company president home. But much more intense than his embarrassment was the compulsion to be alone as soon as possible, to pinch himself with his own fingers to verify whether this tremendous good fortune which he had seized for himself was true or not.

His car came gliding up from beyond the grove. As Kagebayashi was about to get in the car, he noticed Toyama, Chief of the Secretariat, coming up to the driveway.

"Let me see you home," said Toyama, who had seen him about to get into the car. Toyama was a young man whom Otaka had spotted and had promoted successively in an unprecedented way to the position of Chief of the Secretariat at the young age of between thirty and forty. He was said to have the looks and personality of a movie star—the kind of man who got all the girls in the company excited.

Kagebayashi felt rather ticklish about Toyama's escorting him instead of Otaka home. A shrewd fellow, he thought. On the other hand, Kagebayashi could not find fault with Toyama for wanting to go home with him instead of seeing Otaka home. After all, the fact that Otaka had ceased to be the president of the company and he, Kagebayashi, had become the *shacho* could not be known to anyone except the several Directors.

This was something that had just been decided three hours earlier, and the Members of the Board had pledged to keep this fact secret until its formal announcement some three days later. The upcoming reshuffle of personnel could not possibly have reached Toyama's ears. Therefore, if Toyama did know about it, it could only mean that he had independently sensed it through his own intuition.

Actually, that's what had happened in Toyama's case. With the opening of this Emergency General Meeting, it was generally anticipated that there would be some large-scale shifts in personnel, particularly at the upper levels of the company, but no one expected the retirement of Otaka who had come to be known as "the one man for the job." When Otaka was in charge of S——Industries, it was he who made the company as great as it is today. Here, in a year or two, he had founded three new subsidiaries, and it was he in particular who had to take the responsibility for anything that went wrong. However, a thing like Otaka's retirement was something that couldn't happen, not even in a dream. Only to Toyama, however, did the thought occur that this could possibly be the case. Toyama had his own personal way of looking at people, and that was that *anything at all can happen*. That was what he thought of people. Toyama's character had been molded in that direction during his unfortunate childhood. There was the fact that his father had lost his business and committed suicide; there was the fact that his mother had a lover on the side and left home; and there was also the fact that he was taken and supported by a foreigner during his university education—all of these things belonged in his category of *anything at all can happen*.

Seeing Otaka leave his place and Kagebayashi going after him, Toyama had gotten up and left the banquet hall to go along too. He had been unable to sense anything from Otaka's manner. The sullenness that Otaka had manifested seemed no more than his usual unpleasantness, so even though he was in the lowest depths of chagrin, it was impossible to tell that Otaka was unusually sullen.

Kagebayashi also had a similarly sullen expression on his face, but he seemed to be sullen under the pressure of some good fortune of his own. Up until now, Kagebayashi had trained himself in such a way that he could turn on a degree of conviviality in his face even under the most adverse circumstances. So, in Toyama's eyes, Kagebayashi's sullenness connoted something really extraordinary. And it impressed Toyama that Kagebayashi's sullenness was nothing more than powerful sweetness and light—all done up in brown wrapping paper. Toyama knew that he had gained his present position on account of Otaka, but noticing that Kagebayashi was leaving to see Otaka off, he somehow suddenly realized that from now on it behooved him to cut himself off from Otaka and to start getting close to the other fellow. *There's no time like the present to make this switch.*

There was one other person who came to get into the car. It was the younger sister of the proprietress of the restaurant, Teruko. She was a widow and thirty years old this year. There were people who had tried to act as go-betweens in her behalf and had asked around for her, but she was very fastidious, and one by one she had pigeon-holed all discussions of remarriage. On seeing Toyama and Kagebayashi get into the same car, she suddenly took it into her head to tell them that since they were surely both going now to a tea house on the northside, she might as well go along with them.

"Is it all right if I come along too?" asked Teruko, quickly wedging her body, which she always boasted was as resilient as a ball, in next to Kagebayashi.

"Hey! What the hell!" exclaimed Toyama, somewhat flustered. Since he always so excited women, he was in the habit of thinking that the actions and behavior of all women revolved around him as the epicenter of their attention. Even in this instance, there was little doubt in his mind that Teruko had come to get into this car because *he* was there. And that made him feel awkward in front of Kagebayashi.

"It's all right! Toyama-san, be still." Teruko whispered.

"No. It's just impossible today."

"All right then, let's just go and have a drink and talk," said Teruko. Then after a while she turned on a sweetish voice and said, "How about it, *Shacho-san?*"

Toyama gasped. Kagebayashi also gasped, and instantly and unconsciously his body twitched. To Kagebayashi there was an ominous feeling in hearing the young woman distinctly call him *Shacho-san*.

"Tonight is harvest moon. Let's go moon-viewing. What do you say, *Shacho-san?*"

Kagebayashi did not correct her when she referred to him as the company president. Instead, naming a northside tea house, he said, "Toyama, shall we go to Wakimoto's?"

It was harvest moon, but it was cloudy and the moon did not show its face. At Teruko's words, both Kagebayashi and Toyama were peeking out of the car window, and only the driver was impervious to the moon. He was demonstrating his indifference—because there wasn't the slightest tremor in his body.

GOING to Wakimoto's had the character of going on to another party. Up until now, Teruko used to call Kagebayashi Mr. Managing Director or *Kage-sama,* but in the car and from then on she used the term *shacho-san* liberally and without exception. The probability of a personnel shakeup at S——Industries had reached her ears some time back, but when she watched Kagebayashi's manner as he saw Otaka off, Teruko knew that the shakeup had definitely occurred today. Then, on sensing through a well-calculated guess that Kagebayashi might have become president of the company, she had taken a stab at calling him *shacho-san.* Since it was apparent that she had not missed completely, she continued to employ this new appellative even after they arrived at Wakimoto's. Toyama, however, had been more discreet and had not called him *shacho.* Nevertheless, as Teruko persisted in saying "*Shacho-san, Shacho-san,*" Toyama was finding it impossible to continue calling him "Mr. Managing Director."

After getting to Wakimoto's, Kagebayashi, possibly because he felt relieved and relaxed, drank excessively— more than usual. Among his colleagues, he had the reputation of being someone who never became intoxicated, but tonight he got a little drunk, and he himself became aware of this by the wobbling of his legs when he got up to go to the toilet.

When Kagebayashi emerged from the toilet, he thought about the man who had exerted the greatest effort in getting him named to the office of company president and who had been happiest about the final result. This was a Director named Kitazaka. Kagebayashi felt that he just had to invite Kitazaka to this joyous place—today, right now. He had the rather sentimental feeling that he wanted to shake this man's hand and drink a toast with him.

Kagebayashi lifted the receiver of the telephone in the hall and called the southside restaurant. It was the proprietress of the restaurant who answered.

"The party is all over and everybody's just leaving," she said. Kagebayashi, heedless of all the other people there, had her call Kitazaka to the phone and told him where he was.

"Celebrating already?" Pretty fast! said Kitazaka. Then he lowered his voice to a near-whisper and added, "I'm coming right over."

A half hour later there was the sound of a car pulling up, and Kitazaka's flushed face appeared at the door of the room. He looked as serious as usual. On seeing Toyama there, Kitazaka looked at him as though he thought Toyama was out of place there, but otherwise ignoring him, he said, "Pretty fast, huh? Celebrating your presidency, I mean."

Toyama now knew definitely from what Kitazaka had said that Kagebayashi had really been made president of the company. *You see, anything at all can happen.* From then on Toyama also, without compunction, called Kagebayashi *shacho.*

At about that time, the moon appeared for the first time. When the moon came out, a maid opened the sliding doors of the veranda. Various forms of Japanese pampas grass were ornately arranged in a flower vase. Although the other people did not move from their places on the *tatami,* Teruko went out onto the veranda and sat down there to gaze at the moon. At this moment Teruko became clearly aware that she was really in love with Toyama and that she had slipped away from the southside restaurant just to be alone beside him.

The party was getting lively. Four or five young geisha

appeared and surrounded the new company president. The woman who owned the tea house also went over and sat beside him. Kagebayashi was being called *shacho* by everybody. At some point along the line he began to get used to it, and it even began to seem natural for him to be called *shacho*.

"When a man makes money, he starts to want power and rank; after that, women; and when he finds no pleasure even in women, then it's prestige and decorations and honors, huh? What makes me think so is that even a man like President Otaka went blindly after decorations," said Kitazaka.

Kitazaka had joined the company five or six years after Kagebayashi, and in actual age he was in his mid-forties, ten years younger than Kagebayashi, but he looked older than the new *shacho*. He was of a sincere and outspoken nature and never frivolous.

Kagebayashi chimed in with, "Man is a very curious beast," but deep down in his heart, he realized that he—Kagebayashi—actually had always played a role in getting Otaka what he wanted—money, power, women, and decorations. *How I suffered in secret because I tried to protect that man! It was no common ordinary task to be Otaka's wet nurse!* The weight of all those long years of working like a horse under Otaka was suddenly bending the body of the reeling, drunken Kagebayashi.

"Um-h!" Kagebayashi unwittingly let out a little grunt as though he were groaning.

"What are you groaning about?" the proprietress laughed. But Kagebayashi found nothing to laugh about in what had caused him to let out a grunt.

Kitazaka was talking. Kagebayashi's attention was caught when he heard Kitazaka's words vaguely drifting toward him: "So, it ends up that this year's moon-viewing party at Kagiya's has been canceled."

It had been the custom every year for some twenty-odd officers of the company to get together with Otaka and hold a moon-viewing party on the evening of the full moon either in September or October. Kagebayashi would not entrust the management of these banquets to any of the young Division Chiefs or Section Chiefs but always undertook the responsibility himself. There was a reason for not simply fixing the date in either September or October. If it happened to rain on that day, they would certainly incite the displeasure of Otaka. As he did every year when September rolled around, Kagebayashi sent someone to the Weather Bureau to investigate the probable weather conditions; if he found out that it would definitely be clear around that time, they would go ahead with the preparations, but if there was the slightest danger of rain, he would postpone the moon-viewing till October.

This year too, the same as every year, Kagebayashi had turned his attention to the moon-viewing party. When inquiries were made at the Weather Bureau ten days before, they were told that it probably would rain in September around full-moon time, so they had given up and had decided to postpone until October. As it turned out however, instead of raining, it was a beautifully clear day. But it was on that very day that it was unexpectedly decided that Kagebayashi was to become the President of the Company.

Kagebayashi left his place and went out onto the veranda. To Kagebayashi's eyes, the hair at the nape of Teruko's neck, illuminated by the white moonbeams, was mysteriously tantalizing. This was a curious thing for Kagebayashi who had never before permitted his heart to be captured by women.

Then suddenly he heard Toyama's voice. Toyama, who had been talking with Kitazaka, called over to him. "*Shacho,* from now on, to commemorate this night, let's go moon-viewing every year. It would be a pity if the parties came to an end with the end of the Otaka era. So we ought to make a special point of seeing that they continue. What do you say?"

At that instant there suddenly flashed into Kagebayashi's mind a vision of Otaka at Kagiya's in the big hall with its doors removed, majestically holding court at the head of the table at a moon-viewing banquet.

"All right, Toyama. You take over the management of the parties," said Kagebayashi looking up at the September harvest moon which was floating across the clear black sky. *The moon is a beautiful thing indeed.*

That evening there was still another guest at that tea house. He was Jiro Kaibara, a man whose name was known in some quarters because he was a sports commentator and because he contributed columns to the newspapers. He happened to have come to that tea house with a group of newspapermen, but as he was about to leave, he heard that Miyuki Kagebayashi was there, so he decided to poke his head into their room. Kaibara had graduated from a junior high school in a country village at the neck of the A——Peninsula in Aichi Prefecture. Ever since his junior high school days he had been very good at baseball. The fact that he won the championship in the All-Japan Interscholastic Baseball Match when he was a junior in high school ultimately made it difficult for him to divorce himself from baseball for the rest of his life. From the time Kaibara was at B—— University, a private college, he had become famous as an incomparable pitcher, and when he started working for the newspaper, he also acquired renown as a baseball reporter. For a while after the war he had brilliant prospects as the manager of a professional baseball team, but saké was his curse, and it currently appeared that he was out of the running as a top-notch figure and wasn't doing much of anything.

Kaibara had often thought that he would like to meet

the industrialist Miyuki Kagebayashi once, if the opportunity ever presented itself. This was because he knew that Kagebayashi had graduated from the same junior high school as he but eight years earlier and that he had been registered as a member of the same baseball team. He had absolutely no idea how much Kagebayashi had played, but he had decided that it would be a good idea to meet the industrialist who had attended his alma mater before him.

Kaibara had gotten this message across in advance to the proprietress, and in no time at all, this five-foot-ten hulk of a man was sluggishly making his way into Kagebayashi's room.

Kagebayashi also already knew that Kaibara had been a student at his alma mater. When they got to talking about their home town and about their junior high school back home, Kaibara said, "I once played catch-ball with you, *Shacho*. Don't you remember?"

Kagebayashi was surprised. As a university student, when he went home for summer and other vacations he used to go over to the junior high school back home, and there was no denying that he used to play catch-ball with his juniors there; however he had absolutely no recollection of this big fellow's being one of them.

"You had an amazingly fast ball. You were a tough customer to deal with," said Kaibara.

"Really?"

"I'll bet that no one at your company knows about their *shacho*'s varsity days. I don't know too much about them myself—but you sure had a fast ball—really!"

Both Toyama and Kitazaka were amazed by what Kaibara had said. They had never before even thought in terms of a fast speed-ball hurled by the arm of their slender-framed new president. There were also half-credulous, half-sceptical looks on the faces of the proprietress and her geisha.

Kagebayashi thought that Kaibara must have mistaken him for somebody else. However, if there was no reason to correct him, there was also no basis for refuting him.

The night was getting cold, so they closed the sliding doors. From then on, everybody there really began to down the saké in earnest. Teruko, who had been urged to drink indiscriminately by Kaibara, got drunk. She kept calling to Toyama—"Toyama-san, Toyama-san, Toyama-san"—but the fact that he always kept his reserve and did not crumble became terribly exasperating, so with a flaunting air of showing off in front of him, Teruko several times threw herself into the lap of Miyuki Kagebayashi.

III

FROM THE year after Kagebayashi replaced Otaka and took over the reins of the presidency of S——Industries, moon-viewing parties were held annually. During Otaka's regime, the place had been fixed in the southside at Kagiya's, but when Toyama began managing them, places where they would have to stay overnight were always chosen for the moon-viewing parties which were now built around Kagebayashi.

In 1951, they went to Waka-no-ura; in 1952, to Katada on the shore of Lake Biwa. Then from 1953 on, because a large number of officers moved up to Tokyo when the main office was moved there in the spring of that year, places around the Tokyo area were constantly selected for the moon-viewing banquets.

In 1953 they went to Choshi; in 1954, to Mito; in 1955, to Shimoda; and in 1956, to Hakone-Sengokubara. In most cases, acting on the advice of Toyama that he would be tired if he went on the night of the banquet, Kagebayashi left the day before. Normally Kagebayashi was being worked to death just by the pressure of business, and he never took trips except to Osaka or Fukuoka, and for these he traveled only by plane both ways. But once a year he seemed to be able to manage his work so that he could get away just for these annual moon-viewing parties. They continued having these parties ever since Otaka's regime, without ever missing a single year. Kage-bayashi was exceedingly reluctant to disrupt these moon-viewing parties. He reacted toward them as though they were commemorating the fact that there happened to be a harvest moon the day that he assumed the rank of *shacho* in place of Otaka.

Besides that, there was something else. It had been a by-product of these moon-viewing parties and only To-yama and two or three others in the company knew about it, but it provided Kagebayashi with a unique excuse for being able to spend the night with Teruko.

On the night that Kagebayashi became president of the company, Teruko had gotten very drunk and had slept with Kagebayashi, who had been equally as drunk, but this had been completely unanticipated by Teruko. If it had been Toyama with whom she had gone to bed, she could have understood that, but sleeping with Kage-bayashi seemed completely incredible to her. And having sexual relations with Kagebayashi instead of Toyama, whom she loved, radically changed her entire way of thinking with regard to sex. *At any rate, the time when a woman is young is very short. Toyama has a wife and children, and even if I have relations with him, I can't marry him, so maybe it makes sense, after all, to choose President Kagebayashi instead of Mr. Toyama.*

Every month Teruko extracted large sums of money from Kagebayashi. She made herself rationalize that her whole relationship with Kagebayashi was actually for money, but despite that there was also some feeling of attachment and even jealousy over him. When Kagebayashi moved his residence to Tokyo, Teruko also moved —to Kamakura, where she bought about an eighth of an acre of land and built a small house in which she lived with a maid. If Kagebayashi was busy and didn't show up for some days, Teruko became furiously angry. At those times: *I'll just have to pump some more money out of him.* . . .

From Kagebayashi's point of view, thanks to these moon-viewing parties, he could get away on these two-day trips and travel to some unfamiliar place with this young sweetheart of his whom he never could see enough of because of his work, and on these nights of the mid-autumn full moon and the night just preceding, Teruko dragged Kagebayashi from his work and from his family and possessed him exclusively. Generally, on the first night there was a fight and a great tumult over separating or not separating, and on occasion they even had to have Toyama intervene. But by moon-viewing time the next day they were back in a good mood. Kagebayashi would go to the restaurant where the banquet was all set up, and it was late before he returned. Teruko would be by herself on the veranda of the inn, facing the moon. At first Teruko had been bitter and angry over being left to view the moon alone, but at some point she got used to it as though she had been born to do so. There she would be, counting her paper money or manicuring her fingernails, on the veranda where the moonbeams fell. And that was the way she viewed the moon wherever they went; the moon at Waka-no-ura, the moon at Katada, then Choshi, Mito, Shimoda, and Hakone. And all that she knew of all these places was the mid-autumn full moon.

After moving to Tokyo, Kagebayashi attended all of these moon-viewing parties in Japanese-style clothes, just like former president Otaka. Wearing Japanese clothes on these occasions was not the only way in which Kagebayashi was like his predecessor. He had also gradually gotten to be like him in his reticence and in his moodi ness which would alter the color of his face if anything at all displeased him. Fortunately, they did not encounter rain on any of these occasions, but for two successive years, when they were at Choshi and Mito, it was cloudy and the moon showed its face only slightly. And at such times Kagebayashi was frightfully unpleasant.

Generally, through the good offices of Toyama, the proprietress of Wakimoto's was invited up from Osaka to attend these annual banquets. In addition to inviting the proprietress, he also expressly invited and assembled several of the Osaka geisha who were at the banquet the night that Kagebayashi became the *shacho*. The number of geisha decreased year by year. Some of the women had retired as geisha and others had built homes and did not go out as freely as before. And because Kagebayashi even became upset over this, Toyama's problems as the manager of the banquets were multiplied. For Toyama, in addition to his anguish over capricious natural phenomena —such as whether or not the sky would be clear on these days—and his worry over the naturally phenomenal capriciousness with which geisha ran their lives, there was yet another thing connected with these banquets that caused him concern. Ever since the Mito moon-viewing party, the outspoken Kitazaka, fed up with Kagebayashi's "one-man-show" tactics, became reluctant to participate.

"I beg you, please come along, just this one evening," pleaded Toyama.

To this Kitazaka merely replied, "Thanks to Emperor Kagebayashi, you have become a Director so you have to play your role, but I, I'm exempt, huh?"

Toyama had become a Director. As Kitazaka said, his becoming a Director, albeit the lowest ranking one, was solely on Kagebayashi's recommendation. For working for Kagebayashi like a horse and exhausting himself; for going into the kitchen at Kagebayashi's home and fawning over and flattering Kagebayashi's wife; for acting as a buffer between the wife and Teruko; and for being involved in that whole miserable mess—this had been the reward.

One thing that invariably caused the group to get fed up with these moon-viewing parties was the long-windedness of Jiro Kaibara, who had been placed under contract with the company after he became acquainted with Kagebayashi. Every year he retold the same stories about Kagebayashi as an old-timer on his baseball team and the same stories about how nobody, no matter what he did, could get the fast-ball hurled by Kagebayashi when he came to coach the school team.

With his flair for oratory, Kaibara embellished the details of the story every year. Newly-inducted company personnel used to wonder what he was doing in the company, but they listened with interest to the stories by this big man who was known to them as a popular baseball commentator. But after the second year, they thought it would be a nice thing if he just stopped. Kaibara's stories year by year became more and more exaggerated, but they really sounded true. The stories were tinged with a sort of strange excitement as though Kaibara was really reliving those days himself.

Kagebayashi, for his part, never grew weary of hearing Kaibara's stories. By the time Kaibara sat down, Kagebayashi was vividly recalling the glorious days of his youth when he was selected for the baseball team. Before his eyes there even floated visions of Kaibara in baseball uniform unable to manage the speed of his ball.

At the time of the Shimoda party of 1955 a small incident occurred. When Kaibara was telling his stories about baseball, Kitazaka, who was reluctantly attending at Toyama's request, finally got fed up. "Hey! That's enough. Quit your spoofing!" he shouted.

Kaibara scratched his head, started to act like a clown, brought his story to an abrupt end, and returned to his seat. Some of the people studied the face of Kagebayashi, who at that time simply gave the impression that he had not been paying any attention to this. He had silently turned his face toward the veranda, where the gleaming sea could be seen reflecting the moonbeams.

As might have been expected, what Kitazaka had yelled out had cut Kagebayashi to the core. While everyone who had witnessed all this had come to their own conclusions watching him—*oh well, ignorance is bliss*—he was recalling an intolerable situation some years back during President Otaka's era when Kitazaka had revealed a similar lack of self-control and had shouted at one of Otaka's cohorts. Otaka at the time had said nothing but had lifted up a saké cup and, with a gesture as if he were brushing something aside, threw it in the direction of Kitazaka. The cup took a slow curve, went sailing over the heads of several people, caught Kitazaka on the right eyebrow, and fell on the veranda behind him, smashed.

Kagebayashi, still facing the veranda, felt welling up in him a similar impulse to throw a cup now, but he squelched it. He did not understand why he wanted to take revenge on him by throwing a cup as Otaka had done. But Kagebayashi waited for a while until that impulse abated and did not throw the cup. Instead of that, he decided to make Kitazaka a consultant and on that basis ease him out of the company.

Two months after that incident, Kitazaka became a consultant and the following spring he resigned.

Soon after that Kagebayashi noticed that a hostile attitude was developing toward Toyama among the members of the Board of Directors. It appeared that for some time they had been treating Toyama harshly because there was a general concern over the increases in personnel and the over-expansion of business, and they found it impossible to talk with Kagebayashi.

Kagebayashi was expanding the organization at the Kyushu Branch Office, and he thought that he would make Toyama the President of the Branch Office there. This was for Toyama's sake, as well as for Kagebayashi's.

Toyama was extremely dissatisfied with this transfer. He was beginning to hate Kagebayashi who was just using him and was becoming estranged from him. But as ordered, Toyama went to Kyushu as President of the Branch Office. About six months after Toyama assumed this post, however, a charge of breach of faith was raised against Kagebayashi by the labor union at the Kyushu subsidiary. Union Members came up to Tokyo and distributed pamphlets around inside the company. While it could not be charged that Toyama had instigated this, everyone at the Tokyo Main Office felt that Toyama had for some reason condoned it, and he seemed to be watching further developments with great interest.

This being the case, Toyama for the first time did not put in an appearnce at the 1956 moon-viewing banquet in Hakone. Toyama was not there; Kitazaka was not there; the proprietress of Wakimoto's caught a cold and did not come up from Osaka. So in the eyes of everyone, the Sengokubara banquet was a desolate affair.

When the banquet ended, Kagebayashi, accompanied by Kaibara, returned to the inn where Teruko was spending the night. The three of them went out of the inn together and walked for about thirty minutes along the gleaming white moon-lit roads between the residences which were scattered here and there. Because the night air was cold for Kagebayashi, he left Kaibara with Teruko and returned to the inn ahead of them.

On returning to the inn, he caught a glimpse of Teruko's handbag inadvertently lying half-open on the made-up bed. Two match boxes were in evidence, one from Japan Air Lines and the other from an inn in Fukuoka, Kyushu. As Kagebayashi had not been overseeing Teruko's daily life completely, he was then struck with the feeling that for the first time he did not know what on earth she was usually doing.

About thirty minutes later, Teruko returned to the inn.

"When did you go to Fukuoka by plane?" asked Kagebayashi. Teruko was startled and turned pale. On receiving a postcard from Toyama saying that he was not going to the moon-viewing party this year, Teruko knew that she would not be able to go by car with him to wherever the party was to be held as she had done every year until now. She had suddenly realized that she was still as much in love with him as she had been all these years. And she wondered if, after all, it wasn't just to have this drive with Toyama once a year that she even had this sort of relationship with Kagebayashi and had kept it going. Thus reasoning, she had been struck by the feeling that she didn't know what she should do, but she had bought a ticket to Fukuoka and had left Haneda Airport by JAL on the afternoon of the day that she received the postcard.

Toyama had gone to meet her at Fukuoka airport. From there they went together by car to Hakozaki and spent the night at an inn there. And the next day, Toyama went to the Kyushu Branch Office while Teruko headed back to the airport in a separate car. Since her car had traveled along the seacoast, she must gone through Fukuoka, but she had no specific recollection of any place in that city.

For a while, Kagebayashi and Teruko looked daggers at each other, but Teruko quickly regained her composure. She did not believe that Kagebayashi could possibly know of her surreptitious rendezvous with Toyama which had been carried out with such careful precautions. *At worse, somebody may have seen me getting on that plane.*

"I heard there was a good diamond there, and I went

to see it. What's the matter? Why are you looking like that? If you think that's strange and if you don't believe it, then you just think about this for a while. All month long I stay at home alone like somebody on a shelf. What if I did go to buy a diamond?"

Then Teruko lavishly displayed her knowledge of diamonds. For the moment, the greater problem directly involving Kagebayashi was the high price of diamonds that he was hearing bandied about . . . although that did not mean that his doubts about Teruko had been dispelled. But, without further ado, they stopped this fencing and broke off their conversation.

IV

It was in the fall of 1957 that for reasons of a slump in business Kagebayashi was forced to resign from the President's chair at a Big Stockholders' General Meeting. Clearly, people inside and outside the company had gotten together and hatched a plot, but there were no measures he could take to avert this. Finally, the dust went flying. This was inevitable for Kagebayashi who was surrounded by a pack of fawning flatterers among whom was also Toyama. And so it came about that Kagebayashi had to follow the same path as Otaka had before him. Kagebayashi must have had many supporters besides people like the President of the Bank, the President of the Securities Company, and the President of the Insurance Company, who had signatory powers with regard to the company's personnel, but those who would have lent their support to Kagebayashi for some reason did not appear. Seeing that this was the case, there was nothing for him to do but to admit that he had behaved with complete imcompetence. Kagebayashi thought that while the basic cause of all this lay half with himself, the other half lay with Toyama's stratagems. They had not decided who would become the new *shacho*, but they did set a time for his selection, and it looked as though the name of Toyama was appearing on the horizon. There just could not be anyone but Toyama!

It was a week after the Stockholders' General Meeting that Kagebayashi, looking like a *samurai* with his sword broken and his arrows spent, at a Directors' Meeting announced his resolution to resign. When he left the Directors' meeting room and returned to the President's office, he realized the terrible fatigue that was coursing through his body and mind, lowered himself into a chair, and sat there immobile. It appeared that rumors of the *shacho's* resignation were already spreading through all the departments of the company, and there was a different feeling toward Kagebayashi all the way down to the office boys and the girl secretaries.

At seven o'clock, when Kagebayashi ordered the Secretariat to send his car around to take him home, Jiro Kaibara's hulk appeared at the President's office. "Tomorrow is Harvest Moon, so what do we do this year? No notices have gone out," said the stupid baseball commentator. This was also the first time that Kagebayashi had thought about it. The days had flown by without anyone's choosing a place for the moon-viewing party that fall. The business situation was that serious.

The two men left the President's office and got into the automobile in front of the company lobby. Night was falling. The member of the Secretariat who had come down to see him off handled the old *shacho* even more courteously than he usually did and bowed politely. For some unknown reason he seemed to have a strong feeling of respect for the President who would soon be leaving the company.

"Drive to Kamakura," Kagebayashi instructed the driver. He was in no mood to go home. He seemed beguiled by a feeling that only by being beside Teruko could he ease his miserable depression.

The car ran along the Tokyo-Yokohama National Highway. One after another, cars from behind caught up with and passed the car Kagebayashi was in. Because Kagebayashi always disliked going fast, the driver went slowly and hung cautiously onto the steering wheel. When they were crossing Rokugo Bridge, a small bang under the chassis shook the old man's body. The driver stopped the car.

"I'm sorry, but we've got a flat. Please give me about five minutes and wait till I fix it. I really apologize," he said with embarrassment. Kagebayashi knew that his driver had not yet lost his feeling of awe and respect toward him, and for that reason he found it possible to pardon the driver's ineptitude.

The automobile crossed the bridge with the tire flat, and after going on a little further, turned off the highway onto a rice-paddy field. Kagebayashi and Jiro Kaibara both remained silently sitting in the parked car. Kaibara thought that by the time they arrived at Kagebayashi's second home in Kamakura he should be able to consolidate his arguments for setting up an employees' baseball team at the company. This was something that he had been proposing for the past year, at least whenever he met Kagebayashi, but he was never able to get a definite reply. The baseball commentator figured that by having them set up an employees' baseball team at S——Industries, he could solidify his own very insecure standing at the company, where he was just receiving a retaining allowance.

However, Kaibara was born superstitious, and an ill-omened flat tire was not the occasion for broaching this subject, so the better part of wisdom was to forget this talk for today. *But if I keep all this to myself, what's the purpose in my riding in the President's car when he's going to his second home in Kamakura?* When it turned out that he was unable to answer his own question, Kaibara's actions became strikingly peculiar. *I have to talk to him about something!* But nothing intelligent or relevant came into Kaibara's head, as always.

Kagebayashi was also exasperated by the flat. *My car, which did not have a flat even once during my presidency, has to have a flat now that I've stopped being president!* Just as he was thinking this, he for some reason or other became filled by an uneasiness about going to Teruko's house in Kamakura. Whenever he was going down to Teruko's, he always put in a telephone call a few days in advance, but this time his visit was without notice. *Mightn't she not be there? Didn't she go to Fukuoka to buy a diamond?* (Kagebayashi had by now convinced himself that this had been true.) And once this uneasiness reared its head, he began quickly to accept it as established irrefutable truth that Teruko would not be home.

"*Shacho*, your fast-ball was sure hard to get—you know, I don't know anyone with such a fast-ball."

Little by little, the words he had been holding back were coming forward in Kaibara and he was saying them. Kaibara had never said things like this when he was alone with Kagebayashi. This was the first time. This did not mean that what he was now blurting out was just lip service on this occasion. But just because he had so often repeated this same thing over and over again, it had become a reality in his mind now. Kagebayashi was startled by his words. And as if he had discovered something priceless inside a desk drawer, the fast-ball of his student days was now being recalled to him as the only glory that was left to him. That arm of his had pitched fast-balls that were hard for even Kaibara to get—Kaibara, with his big name in baseball.

Kagebayashi opened the door and called out to the driver, "Not yet?"

"It'll be another five minutes." The driver had finished removing the flat tire and was standing holding it. Pushing his hair out of his eyes and back on top of his head while standing holding the tire, he had the appearance of something out of the comics. The driver's shadow was as dark as spilled ink, and the ground was an exceedingly clear, pale blue-white in the moonlight.

Kagebayashi got out of the car and stood on the ground. Then suddenly, in order to whisk away the cold emptiness of the moonbeams which were closing in on him, he swung his right arm forward and up in a large arc. After several decades, Kagebayashi was now again posing in his pitcher's motion. Of course, as a reserve player, he had never had any experience stepping up to the pitcher's mound. But in his current frame of mind, Kagebayashi had forgotten details like that. He arched his body forward, and as though he were actually pitching a ball, he mightily brought down the right arm that he had just swung upward. Because once again he was throwing a fast-ball that even Kaibara would miss.

Inside the car, Jiro Kaibara raised his eyes toward the window and saw something in the shape of a funny old man flinging his emaciated arm around in circles. He sucked in his breath. This figure was ghastly like a phantom devil dancing and bathing in the white rays of the moon which tomorrow would be called the Full Moon.

ALSO AVAILABLE FROM TUTTLE PUBLISHING

THE TALE OF GENJI
by *Murasaki Shikibu*
translated by *Kencho Suematsu*
ISBN 0-8048-3256-0
This biographical novel centers around the amorous exploits of Prince Hikaru Genji, whose elegance and talent epitomized the values of Heian Japan, an era in which indigenous Japanese culture still held prominence over the Chinese culture that would come to dominate Japan.

LITTLE SONGS OF THE GEISHA
Traditional Japanese Ko-Uta
by *Liza Dalby*
ISBN 0-8048-3250-1
A fascinating look into the world of the Geisha through the 400-year-old art of Ko-Uta, the traditional song form sung to three-stringed shamisen music. A vivid evocation of the romanticism of feudal Japan.

THE JOURNEY
a Novel about Japan in the
Aftermath of the American Occupation
by *Jiro Osaragi, translated by Ivan Morris*
ISBN 0-8048-3255-2
This touching allegorical novel about a man who is almost destroyed by his lust for money and the accumulation of wealth is a masterful depiction of the new moral reality facing post-war Japan.

THE BUDDHA TREE
by *Fumio Niwa, translated by Kenneth Strong*
ISBN 0-8048-3254-4
The author's remarkable insight into human weaknesses, his sensitive sketches of the Japanese countryside, and his revelation of the materialism of the modern Buddhist church in Japan, make this a book of unusual distinction.

KAPPA
A Satire By The Author Of Rashomon
by *Ryunosuke Akutagawa,*
translated by *Geoffrey Bownas*
ISBN 0-8048-3251-X
A Swiftian satire of Japanese society thinly disguised as the fictitious Kappaland. Peopled with creatures from Japanese folklore, Kappaland serves as a vehicle for the humorous examination of the moral foibles of Japanese society in the early 20th century.

THE COUNTERFEITER
AND OTHER STORIES
by *Yasushi Inoue, translated by Leon Picon*
ISBN 0-8048-3252-8
These three short stories, "The Counterfeiter," "Obasute," and "The Full Moon," explore the roles of loneliness, compassion, beauty, and forgiveness in day-to-day life in Japan, all within the context of the Buddhist-influenced notion of inescapable predestination.

ROMAJI DIARY AND SAD TOYS
by *Takuboku Ishikawa*
translated by *Sanford Goldstein*
and *Seishi Shinoda*
ISBN 0-8048-3253-6
The novella *Romaji Diary* represents the first instance of a Japanese writer using romaji (roman script) to tell stories in a way that could not be told in kana or kanji. *Sad Toys* is a collection of 194 tanka, the traditional 31-syllable poems that are evocative of Japan's misty past and its tentative steps into the wider world.

FIRES ON THE PLAIN
by *Shohei Ooka, translated by Ivan Morris*
ISBN: 0-8048-1379-5
Based on the author's experience as a prisoner captured by American forces during WWII, *Fires on the Plain* tells the story of the disintegration of Private Tamura, a Japanese soldier during the dark end days of the war. One by one, each of his ties to society is destroyed, until Tamura, a sensitive and intelligent man, becomes an outcast.

THE IZU DANCER
& OTHER STORIES
by *Yasunari Kawabata and Yasushi Inoue*
ISBN 0-8048-1141-5
Four stories from two of Japan's most beloved and acclaimed fiction writers. "The Izu Dancer" was the story that first introduced Kawabata's prodigious talent to the West. Stories by Inoue include, "The Counterfeiter," "Obasute," and "The Full Moon."